Schleiermacher's Interpretation of the Bible

Schleiermacher's Interpretation of the Bible

The Doctrine and Use of the Scriptures in the Light of Schleiermacher's Hermeneutical Principles

IAN S. WISHART

Foreword by Sean J. McGrath

WIPF & STOCK • Eugene, Oregon

SCHLEIERMACHER'S INTERPRETATION OF THE BIBLE
The Doctrine and Use of the Scriptures in the Light of Schleiermacher's
Hermeneutical Principles

Copyright © 2021 Ian S. Wishart. All rights reserved. Except for brief quotations in critical publications or reviews, no part of this book may be reproduced in any manner without prior written permission from the publisher. Write: Permissions, Wipf and Stock Publishers, 199 W. 8th Ave., Suite 3, Eugene, OR 97401.

Wipf & Stock
An Imprint of Wipf and Stock Publishers
199 W. 8th Ave., Suite 3
Eugene, OR 97401

www.wipfandstock.com

PAPERBACK ISBN: 978-1-6667-1378-7
HARDCOVER ISBN: 978-1-6667-1379-4
EBOOK ISBN: 978-1-6667-1380-0

08/31/21

Contents

Foreword by Sean J. McGrath		vii
Preface		ix
1	Introduction and Background	1
	Pietism	6
	The Enlightenment	9
	Scholastic Orthodoxy	13
2	The Psychological Starting Point	16
	Psychology in The Christian Faith	21
	Modification of the Psychological Approach	26
	Summary	29
3	Hermeneutics: Theory and Practice	31
	Interpreting Paul: An Example from *Introduction to the New Testament*	39
	Interpreting Pauline Doctrine	45
4	The Gospels as History	50
	The Christian Faith	51
	Essay on Luke	58
	Introduction to the New Testament: John's Gospel	61
	The Raising of Lazarus	64
	The Resurrection of Christ	68
5	The Use of the Old Testament	73
	The Christian Faith	74
	Creation	79
	Ethics	82
	Summary	87

6	The Church as Interpreter	90
	The Christian Faith	92
	Protestant Tradition Respecting the Lord's Supper	97
	The True Spirit of the Reformation	99
	Correcting the Tradition	101
7	Some Remarks about Schleiermacher's Exegesis	107
	"On Colossians 1:15–20"	109
	Schleiermacher's References to Romans 8	115
	Schleiermacher's Use of Sermon Texts	120
8	The Problem of Authority	124
	The Reversal of Method	125
	The Doctrine of the Holy Spirit	129
	The Proclamation of Christ	134

Conclusions — 138

Concluding Unscientific Postscript, 2021 — 141
    Schleiermacher's Use of His Own Hermeneutic — 141

Selected Bibliography — 143
    Works by Friedrich Schleiermacher — 143
    Works by Other Authors — 145

Foreword

Sean J. McGrath
Professor of Philosophy and Theology, Memorial University of Newfoundland

IAN WISHART'S STUDY OF the sermons of Friedrich Schleiermacher stands in sharp contrast to that of Karl Barth given almost a century ago.[1] Barth had little time for the hermeneutics, and even less time for the transcendental psychology of the father of Protestant Liberalism. Wishart, recognizing Schleiermacher's contribution to both these fields, reads Schleiermacher's sermons as complimentary to his hermeneutics and psychology. Since Schleiermacher is better known today as a hermeneutician and a transcendental thinker than he is as preacher, Wishart's approach will be eye-opening to many.

At the heart of Schleiermacher's theology, Barth sees a tension between two apparently irreconcilable commitments: on the one hand, Schleiermacher's commitment to transcendental idealism (from Kant to Schelling), and on the other, his equally strong commitment to the historically contingent, irreducible revelation of the Christ.[2] Ian Wishart discerns a similar tension in Schleiermacher, but rather than seeing it, as Barth does, as detrimental for Schleiermacher's theology, Wishart reads the tension as the creative source of Schleiermacher's vitality. There are, of course, many Schleiermachers—the hermeneutical Schleiermacher, the psychological Schleiermacher, the Schleiermacher who translates Plato and recognizes truth in other religions as well as in the apparently irreligious ("the culture

---

1. Barth, *Theology of Schleiermacher*, 3–134.
2. Barth, *Theology of Schleiermacher*, 105.

despisers" for whom he wrote his first book).³ But for Wishart, they all seamlessly converge in Schleiermacher the theologian, who preached most Sundays of his adult life. As Wishart shows us in this masterful book, Schleiermacher's message from the pulpit was not primarily apologetic. It was rather soteriological. For all his syncretistic leanings, Wishart points out how Schleiermacher remains committed to the singularity of the redemptive event of the incarnation. And even if the subject matter of theology is, according to the mature Schleiermacher, the Christian self-reflection on the consciousness of this event, an event it remains, a happening in history, which like any event is not reducible to its effects on subjectivity.

Schleiermacher worked out his mature theology in the context of reading Scripture as a historical document, written by human beings remote from us in time and place. This meant that theology was essentially hermeneutical or interpretive. The reader of Scripture must be conscious of the historical gap that separates the understanding of the authors of Scripture from his or her own time, and deploy a method for traversing that gap. Others had said similar things before. Schleiermacher, however, was the first to recognize that the hermeneutical predicament of the theologian is also the predicament of human understanding in general. To understand is to interpret, and to interpret is to translate, or as Gadamer put it, to fuse horizons.⁴ Regardless of whether or not we take the goal of interpretation to be the understanding of the perspective of the other, as Schleiermacher does, or the understanding of the thing meant, as Gadamer does, to interpret is always to understand what a text means and can mean for us today.⁵

Ian Wishart shows us a Schleiermacher who works out his hermeneutical theory in practice, by joyfully embracing his duty as a pastor and preaching the gospel every Sunday, with the aim of helping his parishioners understand what is perennially true about it, if only by better recognizing what is historical contingent in it, and perhaps even no longer relevant. Just like Barth himself, we will never be finished reading Schleiermacher. Wishart's book offers us a timely opportunity to revisit in depth the preaching of the greatest theologian of the nineteenth century.

3. Friedrich Schleiermacher, *On Religion* 1988 (Ueber die Religion 1799).

4. Hans-Georg Gadamer, *Truth and Method*. Second Revised Edition. Trans. Joel Weinsheimer and Donald G. Marshall (New York: Continuum, 1995), 306–7.

5. See Heidegger, "Phenomenological Interpretations in Connection with Aristotle," 112.

Preface

How is a text to be understood? How does understanding itself occur?

These questions lie at the heart of Schleiermacher's theory of interpretation, his hermeneutics.[1]

Understanding is a mysterious phenomenon, yet known to all. It remains the central concern of hermeneutics.[2]

Schleiermacher's New Testament hermeneutics is to guide and aid exegesis. . . . Amidst the welter of detail, however, it is important to keep clearly in view that the ultimate goal is to understand fully the unique messages set forth in the New Testament texts.[3]

THE PRESENT STUDY OF Schleiermacher's interpretation of the Bible was written for Knox College, Toronto, in 1968. At the time, there was very little published concerning his hermeneutics, either in English or in German. Karl Barth's *Die Theologie Schleiermachers* was published in 1978, and its English translation appeared in 1982.[4]

Barth's intense interest in Schleiermacher began when he reviewed a book by Emil Brunner. Brunner had been appointed to the faculty of the University of Zürich in 1921 and published a critique of the theology of

---

1. Duke, "Translator's Introduction," 1.
2. Duke, "Translator's Introduction," 15.
3. Duke, "Translator's Introduction," 8.
4. Karl Barth, *Karl Barth Gesamtausgabe, Die Theologie Schleiermachers*; Barth, *Theology of Schleiermacher*.

Friedrich Schleiermacher. Barth agreed with Brunner's general position, but criticized Brunner's neglect of Schleiermacher's preaching. Brunner replied in a second edition of his book *Die Mystik und das Wort*,[5] and noted the complaint. Brunner regarded it as legitimate to deal with scientific writing independently of what he regarded as more casual works. He acknowledged that his judgment of Schleiermacher was one-sided, derived from the latter's use of various levels of speech—sometimes religious, sometimes poetical or rhetorical or scientific. He maintained that Schleiermacher's sermons were equivocal in meaning, showing a struggle in his thought between two heterogeneous elements: a mystical system of identity philosophy and the Christian faith.

Brunner's attack points to a major question raised from all sides by those dealing with Schleiermacher's thought: What is the relative importance of psychological and historical principles in his writings? For the history of theology in the nineteenth century, it is clear that it was his psychological principles which gained attention. This was the side of his thought which was most original and provocative in expression. It was the *Addresses on Religion* and *The Christian Faith* which made him famous; his exegetical work is largely unread, much of it still unpublished. However, for a balanced view of Schleiermacher's own position, a greater emphasis must be given to the historical side of his thought than has generally been the case.

The person who complained of Brunner's procedure was Karl Barth. At the time, Barth was lecturing on Schleiermacher's sermons at Göttingen in the winter semester of 1923–24. Barth acknowledged that Brunner's book spurred his own response to Schleiermacher. However, his own critique started with the sermons and proceeded with a broad approach to Schleiermacher as a preacher, as a theologian, and as a man. Barth praised Brunner's book when he reviewed it, generally agreeing with Brunner's attack. About the same time, he had written to a friend that he planned to declare war on Schleiermacher. In his lectures on the sermons, he was severely critical of their theology; the lectures opened "an assault that would continue unhindered for many years."[6] However, in the "Concluding Unscientific Postscript," the afterword written forty-five years after his declaration of war, Barth's scorn was modified by respectful appreciation for the greatest theological thinker of the nineteenth century.

Reflecting on Schleiermacher's personality and life's work, Barth observed that there is no one "whose calibre and stature would be worthy of

---

5. Brunner, *Die Mystik und das Wort*, 361–66.
6. Ritschl, "Editor's Preface," ix.

mention in the same breath with those of Schleiermacher."[7] This appreciation was coupled with the enduring rejection of Schleiermacher's theology.

Barth's opinion was that Schleiermacher was first of all a pastor, then a professor, and last of all a philosopher.[8] First, he was a pastor, a preaching pastor, and preached every Sunday for years. Barth made an intense and extensive examination of Schleiermacher's sermons in the final years of the latter's life, together with special examination of his preaching on festal occasions like Christmas, Good Friday, and Easter. No ordinary preacher will ever have had his or her work examined so thoroughly! Schleiermacher's output was huge, and Barth dealt only with a portion of it. The lectures on preaching comprise the first half of Barth's book *The Theology of Schleiermacher*. The book contains the series of lectures delivered at the University of Göttingen in the winter of 1923–24. The second half deals with other material, *The Encyclopedia, Hermeneutics, The Christian Faith*, and *Speeches on Religion*.

The chapter on hermeneutics is unsatisfactory, referring only to a small section of Schleiermacher's writing on the topic. Barth commented that Schleiermacher "triumphantly deals with the ancient doctrine of inspiration," a general remark which did not deal with Schleiermacher's detailed interpretation of biblical texts.[9] The headings of the two parts of Schleiermacher's *Hermeneutic und Kritik* are listed with the notation "dropped," an indication that Barth did not have time in his course of lectures to deal with them. Barth's own views on hermeneutics are best outlined in *Church Dogmatics* I/2 and III/3, where he does not even mention Schleiermacher. For Schleiermacher, the interpretation of literary texts and the theory of interpretation are of utmost importance. The present study endeavors to give them their due.

In the present study, primary attention is given to Schleiermacher's later writings. The balance of psychology and history is more readily seen in the works of his mature period. In this period, both the first and second editions of *The Christian Faith*[10] appeared, as well as the works on New Testament interpretation and most of the published sermons. In 1817,

---

7. Barth, *Theology of Schleiermacher*, 274.
8. Barth, *Theology of Schleiermacher*, xviii.
9. Barth, *Theology of Schleiermacher*, 183.
10. Schleiermacher, *Der christliche Glaube*; Schleiermacher, *Christian Faith* (1963, translation of the second German edition). This work is arranged in 170 numbered divisions in two volumes, and each division is divided into numbered subdivisions of varying length. The present study references the 1963 English translation of the work. Division and subdivision numbers are indicated in parentheses for ease of referencing other editions.

Schleiermacher wrote his lectures on *Christian Ethics*[11] and published the *Essay on Luke*.[12] Two years later came his lectures on hermeneutics[13] and the article "On the Characteristic Value and Binding Aspect of Symbolic Books,"[14] followed in 1820 by the first edition of *The Christian Faith*. "The Homilies on John's Gospel"[15] were delivered between 1823 and 1826, during which period the article "On the Difference between Natural and Moral Law"[16] also appeared. *The Introduction to the New Testament*[17] was a series of lectures which are dated 1829, with later revisions. Most of the sermons consulted have been from the last ten years of Schleiermacher's life, those on the Augsburg Confession having been delivered in 1830, and a full collection of his preaching from 1831–34 having been included in the *Collected Works*.[18] Also from the later years come the "Letters to Dr. Luecke on The Christian Faith,"[19] and the essay "On Colossians 1:15–20."[20] Brief reference is made to some of Schleiermacher's letters,[21] and to two of his earlier works, namely the *Addresses on Religion*[22] (1799) and the *Brief Outline on the Study of Theology*[23] (1811). Principal attention is given to *The Christian Faith* as the central expression of Schleiermacher's later theology, but the attempt is

11. Schleiermacher, *Friedrich Schleiermachers saemmtliche Werke*, part I, vol. 12, *Die christliche Sitte*. Subsequent references to the multivolume work use the abbreviation *Saemmtliche Werke*. In the text, this publication is referred to as *Collected Works*.

12. *Saemmtliche Werke*, part I, vol. 2, *Ueber die Schriften des Lukas / Ueber den sogenannten ersten Brief des Paulos an den Timotheus*.

13. *Saemmtliche Werke*, part I, vol. 7, *Hermeneutik und Kritik mit besonderer Beziehung auf das Neue Testament*.

14. *Saemmtliche Werke*, part I, vol. 5, *Ueber den eigenthuemlichen Werth und das bindende Ansehen symbolischer Buecher*.

15. *Saemmtliche Werke*, part II, vols. 8–9, *Ueber das Evangelium des Johannes*.

16. *Saemmtliche Werke*, part III, vol. 2, *Ueber den Unterschied zwischen Naturgesez und Sittengesez*.

17. *Saemmtliche Werke*, part I, vol. 8, *Einleitung ins neue Testament*.

18. *Saemmtliche Werke*, 31 vols. This collection was published in three divisions: theology, sermons, and philosophy and related subjects. In the text, this publication is referred to as *Collected Works*.

19. *Saemmtliche Werke*, part I, vol. 2, *Ueber seine Glaubenslehre an Herrn Dr. Luecke*.

20. *Saemmtliche Werke*, part I, vol. 2, *Ueber Kolosser 1:15–20*.

21. *Aus Schleiermachers Leben in Briefen*. The first two volumes are translated into English in *The Life of Schleiermacher as Unfolded in His Autobiography and Letters*. Subsequent footnotes reference the English translation.

22. Schleiermacher, *Ueber die Religion*. This is a text of the first German edition with the original pagination.

23. *Saemmtliche Werke*, part I, vol. 1, *Kurze Darstellung des theologischen Studiums*; Schleiermacher, *Brief Outline on the Study of Theology* (translation of the second German edition).

made to see Schleiermacher's principles as outlined in this work in the light of his exegesis and his preaching, rather than the reverse.

Barth's lectures on Schleiermacher's sermons were, it bears repeating, not published in German until 1978, or in English until 1982,[24] and like his *Die Theologie Schleiermachers*, were not available when this study was written in 1968.

Hermeneutics was an aspect of Schleiermacher's thought which should never be omitted in a study of his preaching, his theology, and his philosophy.

---

24. See footnote 4 above.

1

Introduction and Background

INTERPRETATION OF THE BIBLE is often considered to be the task of communicating the message of the Scriptures in an age whose thought and common life have little in common with ancient Palestine. The problem of communication is a problem of media: Should the church not employ modern media of data-processing and electronic systems to reshape the minds of men and women in conformity with the Christian ethic, or should the individual Christian not conclude that the time for words is past, and by direct action demonstrate what God's love for suffering humankind may mean in some particular area of human life?

Schleiermacher, long before the age of McLuhan or Leger, had thought deeply about the problems of communicating the gospel and the medium of communication, and he had an answer set out in principle which he elaborated in his own practice. The church lives by preaching; in proclamation a Christian gives expression to the personal consciousness of God, and, insofar as being an official spokesperson of the church, gives expression to the common consciousness of the Christian community. This proclamation germinates in the consciousness of the hearer, stimulates there a consciousness of God, of sin and redemption, and issues in action, which is the ethical result of faith.

For Schleiermacher, there is a deeper problem than that of communication involved in the task of interpretation. This is the problem of understanding. Interpretation seen as communication is an active proceeding;

seen as understanding, it is a receptive task. Hearing the proclamation of the gospel does not necessarily result in understanding; reading the text of the Bible does not necessarily issue in faith. Understanding is the result of conscious intention, a fact that we often overlook when we read or listen. Because the New Testament is written in Greek, the Old Testament in Hebrew, and the thought forms of both are foreign to us, we are forced to face consciously the problem of understanding with respect to them. However, the necessity of constant translation from the thought-pattern of one person to that of another is, in Schleiermacher's view, necessary for the understanding of all communication, even in such simple examples as reading a letter or engaging in conversation. This work of translation is the essential basis of understanding, and the principles by which it proceeds are the principles of hermeneutics.

Schleiermacher regarded the task of interpreting the New Testament as the same, in principle, as the task of interpreting any other literary work. Because of its nature as a work written by Jewish authors living in a Hellenistic world, it has peculiar problems associated with it, requiring special hermeneutical solutions. Because of its nature as the expression of apostolic faith, it has a unique place which sets it apart from all other writings. However, the problem of interpreting it is a problem of understanding. To understand it, we must learn its language and structure, the circumstances of its composition and transmission, the purposes for which it was written, and the meaning which it had for those who wrote it and for those who read it. We need to study the New Testament extensively and intensively, learning the grammatical and historical details about its composition, and also the inner characteristics which make the book unique. Schleiermacher rejected the idea of interpreting the New Testament in the light of an exterior dogmatic principle of unity in thought and composition. He sought to understand the various New Testament authors individually, yet behind them to see a larger unity which was the life they shared in common, the life and spirit of Christ.

This study is concerned with Schleiermacher's interpretation of the Bible. As such, it is the interpretation of an interpretation, an attempt to understand the biblical understanding of a nineteenth-century theologian. It is an attempt to deal with one aspect of his thought in accordance with his own principles. As a result, it is necessary to place this aspect of his thought in the setting of his life and general theology. Schleiermacher's interpretation of the Bible was not an accidental circumstance of his life, nor a casual aspect of this thought: when he was speaking of the Bible, he was not talking about the weather. To understand his approach to interpretation, it is necessary to remember that Schleiermacher was a professional theologian, not of the kind whose whole attention is taken by the building of a system, but one who was concerned with philosophy and general literature, who was active in political life at a time of revolutionary change, who took part in the public leadership of the church, and who preached most Sundays of his life, from the time when he came to Berlin as a young man until his death thirty-eight years later. Biblical interpretation was a very practical task, grounded in the necessities of classroom and pulpit. But it was no mere professional task. Dogmatics and preaching were both founded on the proposition that they gave expression to the true thought of their author; both were essentially functions of the church, whereby it transmitted its message of faith. Thus, Schleiermacher's interpretation is an exposition of his own religion, a personal testimony to his faith, and a part of his attempt to communicate that faith both to his fellow Christians and to the cultured despisers of all religion.

In principle, a proper consideration of Schleiermacher would deal with all sides of his life, and within it seek to outline the productive center of thinking and the method which leads from the central conceptions to secondary thoughts.

An *extensive* treatment of Schleiermacher's writing has never been attempted, most interpreters being content to confine their attention to a narrow group of works on general theology and philosophy. This study cannot deal with all of Schleiermacher's writing, not even with all he wrote about the Bible, but it does attempt to bring some of his lesser-known works into the discussion of his theology. An *intensive* examination of his principles also presents problems of great difficulty. The seminal concepts of his thinking are not easily identified, although several authors confidently claim to have isolated them. With respect to his interpretation of the New Testament, his concept of proclamation is one which ought to be in the center of the discussion, yet it is frequently ignored. However, the discussion is not closed, and will continue for a long time to come. In particular, his exegesis of the New Testament is a topic which needs further development: it is hoped that this study may open the subject a little; it certainly will not close the discussion. Ten volumes of his sermons constitute one section of his *Collected Works*, and other volumes contain such of his exegetical works as have been published, yet most discussions of his work do not even acknowledge this material in the bibliography.

The general question raised with respect to Schleiermacher's thought concerns the relationship between his philosophy and theology, and the extent to which his true allegiance was given to each. Is his thought to be considered a contribution to the literature of the history of religion, or as a theology truly submissive to the message of Christian revelation? Is his system the development of a psychology of religion, or are its leading ideas theological in character, based on the gospel? Was Schleiermacher an artist of the romantic school who used biblical ideas to paint any picture he liked, with the same freedom as a painter of canvas, or was he an earnest preacher who sought to translate the gospel message into such terms that its challenge would be heard and acknowledged in nineteenth-century Germany? Is Schleiermacher's religion simply the working out of his own feelings, or is it an expression of a genuine faith in Christ, in whom we meet God entirely outside of ourselves? Was Schleiermacher's interpretation of the New Testament *eisegesis*, the arbitrary reading of his own ideas into the text of the Bible, or was it *exegesis*, the painstaking effort to read the New Testament in such a way that it truly expresses the word of God? These questions are not answered, for in the end the answer is beyond our judgment. Schleiermacher was deeply aware of these questions, and of the questionable nature of any attempt to use human speech with respect to God. He acknowledged that any theologian runs the risk of putting himself in the place of God. The question which is raised against his theology is the question raised against every other theologian's system.

With particular reference to his biblical interpretation, the basic question is that which is raised about his whole system: Does his philosophical or his theological interest prevail? One form of the question concerns his differing treatment of the Old and New Testaments. It will be seen that Schleiermacher is unable to make any positive use of the Old Testament in his system of thought. The Old Testament is dismissed in Schleiermacher's system as a relic of a more primitive age, retained for merely historical reasons, but of no more intrinsic importance than many works outside the canon. His view of the Old Testament depends, in part at least, on a concept of the developing "history of religions," in which outmoded religious ideas are discarded with the advance of human progress. If this is really characteristic of his general idea of religious development, why does a similar procedure not obtain with respect to the New Testament and to Christ? Some interpreters think that the same principle does apply in both cases, and that further human advancement would mean for Schleiermacher that Christ himself had become outmoded. Schleiermacher denied this on numerous occasions, never more charmingly than in one of the sermons of his later years:

> For a long time there has been a fable among men, and even in these days it is frequently heard. Absent faith has delighted in it, and weak faith has accepted it. It runs this way: A time is coming, perhaps it is here already, when even to this Jesus

of Nazareth justice will be done. Each human memory is fruitful only for a certain time. The human race has much to thank him for. God has achieved great things through him. But even so, he was only one of us and the hour must strike in which he will be forgotten. Was he really serious in wishing to make the world entirely free? Then it must have been his will to make it free of himself, so that God might be all in all. Then men would know that they have power enough in themselves to fulfill the divine will. Moreover, knowing the divine will correctly they would be able to go beyond its limits whenever they wished. Yes, when first the Christian name is forgotten, then will arise the universal kingdom of love and truth, in which no seed of enmity will remain, such as has been sown from the beginning between those who believe in Jesus and the remaining children of men. This fable is not true! Since the days of his flesh the picture of the Redeemer has been indelibly imprinted on the human race! Even if the letters were to disappear, letters which are no more than holy because they verify this picture for us, the picture itself will remain forever. Too deeply is it engraved in men for it ever to be effaced. What the disciple says will always be true: Lord, where should we go? You alone have the words of eternal life![1]

The problem of the relationship of Old and New Testaments may also be formulated in the reverse direction. Christ is the fixed center of faith, whose action and speech are the expression of an absolutely perfect God-consciousness, and in response to whom Christian preaching arises. The New Testament is the necessary and sufficient norm by which to measure all expressions of the Christian self-consciousness. The Holy Spirit, as the spirit of the New Testament, ensures that no expression of Christian faith will be set forth in terms which are incompatible with the New Testament. Why then could an extension of this principle not have made the Old Testament into a constructive instrument of faith? Why is the Holy Spirit not present in the Old Testament as he is in the New?

The differing value given to the Old and New Testaments and the relationship of the Holy Spirit to each of the two sections of the Bible is one of the most important—if not central—problems of Schleiermacher's interpretation of the Bible. This study is an attempt to answer it, and to deal with the following questions which arise from modern criticisms of Schleiermacher's theology. Schleiermacher regards the Bible as a human book. Must this mean that the center of gravity of his thought lies with humanity? The human

---

1. Schleiermacher, *Saemmtliche Werke*, part II, vol. 3 (*Predigten*), 10.

self-consciousness is the starting point for Schleiermacher's exposition of doctrine, but is it true that his theology is based on the single principle of self-awareness, concerned alone with itself, and does the subjective center of thought absorb and destroy all objective references? What is the source of Schleiermacher's conception of Christ? Is it the historic record of the gospel, or simply his own *Weltanschauung*? Does the historical Christ of the New Testament recede more and more into the background of Schleiermacher's thought, its place to be taken by tradition, so that his system is really more akin to that of the Roman Catholic Church than to that of Protestantism? Where is the locus of authority in his theology? Before dealing with these questions, it is necessary first to inquire about the background of his biblical interpretation. In what way is his interpretation of the Bible an outgrowth of the religious and intellectual movements of his day? Specifically, what were the several ways in which pietism, rationalism, and Protestant orthodoxy affected his approach to the Bible?

PIETISM

Schleiermacher's roots in pietism were very deep. Pietism was a widespread movement among the German Protestant churches, a movement inspired by the writing of Philip Jakob Spener at the end of the seventeenth century—and aimed at the achievement of Christian perfection through ascetic practices.[2] One of the branches of pietism was the Moravian Brotherhood, which was organized as a separate church at Herrnhut in 1727. As a boy, Schleiermacher was educated at Moravian schools, first at Niesky and subsequently at Barby, which was the Moravian seminary for ministers.

Schleiermacher begins *The Christian Faith* with the concept of piety.[3] The essential business of the church is the maintenance, regulation, and advancement of piety. Piety is human activity directed against the world, where the world is taken to be all existence and activity apart from the work of the kingdom of God. Piety is a separation from the activities of human knowledge and human power, a retreat from science and politics. This is part of Schleiermacher's conception of religion as grounded in feeling, apart from knowledge and action. Thus, despite Schleiermacher's desire that faith communicate with culture, his pietism lies at the heart of his theological system. For the pietists, the Bible was the main vehicle of their withdrawal from the world. The first point of Spener's program was the gathering together of small groups for Bible reading and personal counsel. The Bible

---

2. For a discussion of Spener, see M'Giffert, *Protestant Thought Before Kant*, 155–61.
3. Schleiermacher, *Christian Faith*, vol. 1 (3:1), 5.

was regarded as a practical book, one which should be open and put to use. It was also a book which was readily understood; it could be used regularly and directly by people who had no training in literary subjects, languages, or history. Schleiermacher accepted the first point without acknowledging the second. The Bible is a book for practical use in the church. The opening of the Bible was one of the three major points for which we stand in debt to the Reformation.[4] But the Bible is not uniformly understandable; it requires interpretation based on careful study of the text, church history, and present Christianity. To that interpretation he dedicated his life in preaching, lecturing, and writing.

On the basis of their Bible reading and personal counsel, the pietists sought to evoke experience which would lead to practical service. By experience they frequently meant moments of emotion, visions, and conversions. John Wesley reported that his heart was "strangely warmed" at a Moravian meeting in London in 1738. Their service has been the inspiration of many Christian groups who know nothing about the movement. They were among the first Protestant groups to send missionaries abroad to work among non-Christian people. Their children's schools and institutions for the care of the unfortunate were the models of such places for two centuries. These tendencies were represented in Schleiermacher's theology by his strong emphasis on experience and on ethics.

Like Aquinas before him, Schleiermacher was a theologian of experience. Experience, not speculation, must be the basis of every doctrine and of the system itself. By experience, he did not mean emotional transport but rather the universal experience, found in all humankind, of the feeling of absolute dependence. Experience was the ground of faith, and faith was the ground of action. In his system, an ethical demand was implicit in every expression of faith, and systematic ethics was the correlative of systematic doctrine. He interpreted the Bible in these terms. The books of the New Testament are a witness to faith, a response to the experience of the disciples of being with Christ. The working out of faith is found in the ethics of daily living, whether in nationalistic response to the invasion of a foreign army, or in the domestic problems concerned with marriage.

An example of such practical application of the Bible is found in the series of sermons which Schleiermacher preached, in 1818, on the Christian household.[5] In the preface to the published version of the sermons, he

---

4. "On the Augsburg Confession," *Saemmtliche Werke*, part II, vol. 2 (*Vierte-Siebente Sammlung*), 626–37.

5. Schleiermacher, "Predigten ueber den christlichen Hausstand," *Saemmtliche Werke*, part II, vol. 1 (*Erste-Dritte Sammlung*), 551–672; Schleiermacher, *Selected Sermons*, 146–83.

expressed the hope that they would serve to stimulate piety in the home life of readers. Three sermons in the series are devoted to the raising of children; in these sermons, Schleiermacher explains that the aim of Christian education is to make children receptive for the working of the divine Spirit. In order to do so, children should be told of the blessings of God, and of the gift of the Redeemer, as early as possible:

> For what is gained if the Spirit of God is not awakened in their hearts? Until this occurs the care and trouble of the teacher has not arrived at its goal. Only then are the powers we have aroused and used brought to their true master; only then can we rejoice that for the first time our youth have taken their places as members of the Christian community in their own right, are seen to be working with us and near us. That no nurture can effect this we all know well. But one may ask, does this not extend beyond the boundaries of nurture, in fact beyond the boundaries of all human capability.... But with this acknowledgment of our own powerlessness, let us not forget that the same Redeemer, who said that the Spirit blows where he wills, also commanded his disciples to go forth and to teach all people.... What is within our power and what also we are commanded to do, is that in our daily lives among our youth we praise the great acts of God. Thus, we seek to raise up the desire for a more holy condition of men through which the divine Spirit may be unlocked in their hearts, and to arouse the dispositions of the young in this way. This is precisely what the apostle called bringing them up in the admonition of the Lord.[6]

These sermons were preached on a series of texts from the New Testament, with particular reference to Ephesians. They are an example of Schleiermacher's desire to make the Bible come alive in the daily living of Christian people, which was part of his heritage from the Moravians.

Schleiermacher was repelled by the anti-intellectualism of the Moravian church. The seminary training was devoted to the development of sentimental piety; contemporary science, philosophy, and poetry were forbidden reading to the students. Schleiermacher's desire to read and understand contemporary intellectual movements resulted in his expulsion from the seminary (lest he corrupt the other students). He proceeded to the University of Halle and steeped himself in the philosophy of Kant. In succeeding years, he made himself a central figure in the intellectual and cultural life of Prussia, and he sought to commend faith to the leading cultural circles of

---

6. *Saemmtliche Werke*, part II, vol. 1 (*Erste-Dritte Sammlung*), 620–21; Schleiermacher, *Selected Sermons*, 163.

his time. But his religion continued to have strong elements of pietism in its makeup, and his desire for practical rather than speculative interpretation of the Bible was one of these. He acknowledged the debt. In a letter to his sister, written from Barby in later years, he included a sentence which is one of his most-quoted remarks:

> There is no place which revives, as this does, the living recollection of the entire movement of my mind, from the first awakening to better things up to the point where now I stand. It was here that the consciousness of the relation of man to a higher world was first stirred within me . . . It was here that the mystic tendency, which has been so essential to me, first developed itself—a tendency that has saved and sustained me amidst all the storms of scepticism. Then it was only a germ, now it is matured; and I can say, after all that has happened, that I am still a Herrnhuter—only a Herrnhuter of a higher order.[7]

THE ENLIGHTENMENT

Schleiermacher's second intellectual home was the Enlightenment.[8] The German phase of the general movement of European rationalism, which had included English Deism and the French philosophes, was in its decline during the early years of Schleiermacher's life. Characteristic of the Enlightenment had been its general rejection of revelation and the elevation of reason to the central place in life and thought. In many cases, this involved a thoroughgoing rejection of religion, but some writers attempted to make a place for Christianity within the rationalistic framework. Rationalistic religion had one fixed principle: nothing could be accepted which was contrary to reason; reason was thus the first principle of religion—and revelation, if it was to be accepted at all, must conform to and be judged by the standards of reason.

The effects of such thinking upon the understanding of the Bible were profound, and its influence upon Schleiermacher is very apparent. He is unable to affirm the Bible as revelation, and even less to assert that Christian doctrine can be designated as revealed. Thus, at the beginning of his interpretation of the Bible, he rejects the concept of Christian truth basic alike to the doctrinal traditions of Protestantism and Roman Catholicism.

---

7. *Life of Schleiermacher*, vol. 1, 200.

8. See the article entitled "Aufklaerung" in Galling, *Die Religion in Geschichte und Gegenwart*, vol. 1.

Both sides of the division within Western Christianity had affirmed the revealed nature of the propositions of Christian belief; in the Roman Catholic Church, divine truth was found as a deposit of faith in Scripture and tradition, whereas the Protestant position was that this dignity applied to Scripture alone. Schleiermacher denies that the term "revelation" can be applied to any propositions, whether scriptural or traditional. In *The Christian Faith*, his discussion of revelation is based on his distinction between facts and propositions. This is one of a series of interrelated distinctions which appear at various places in his works: feeling and knowledge, experience and reason, faith and doctrine, the suprarational and the rational, the given and the content of reflection. In each case, the second element in the distinction is some aspect of human language and expression. Language is a human activity to be constructed and judged by human standards. As such, it cannot be revelation. If revelation is thus not a matter of language and doctrine, it is not a term properly applied to the Bible.

Schleiermacher's discussion of revelation was not the answer of rationalism to the problem, but it was one which depended on the whole rationalistic attack on revealed doctrine. Its effect upon Christian teaching was quite as far-reaching as the rationalist position itself. Immediately the Bible lost its place as the object of faith, and became instead a witness to Christ. No longer was it sufficient to ascertain what the Bible taught on some particular matter, whether of doctrine or of history. It was now proper and necessary to ask when and why something was said in the Bible, and then to judge whether it could be regarded as correct and applicable in modern times.

E. G. Kraeling traces Schleiermacher's general doctrine of Scripture to Lessing.[9] In particular, he traces three of Schleiermacher's basic ideas to him. First, the Scriptures are not the basis of faith in Christ, but our acceptance of the Scriptures is based on such faith.[10] This, Schleiermacher designates as his first doctrine of the Scriptures, and its appearance in a work of dogmatics constituted a revolution for Protestant theology. Schleiermacher acknowledges this revolutionary character, admitting that the exact reverse is the standard opinion of Protestant orthodoxy. Secondly, the New Testament Scriptures are to be regarded as the first and authoritative presentation of Christian faith.[11] This is the natural development of Schleiermacher's conception of revelation with respect to the Bible. If the Scriptures are not revelation, then their dignity must be attained as a witness to

---

9. Kraeling, *Old Testament Since the Reformation*, 60.
10. *Christian Faith*, vol. 2 (128), 591.
11. *Christian Faith*, vol. 2 (129), 594.

faith. Thirdly, the New Testament writings are authentic in that they were produced among the circles influenced by the Holy Spirit, which proceeded from Jesus.[12] Schleiermacher discusses this aspect of the doctrine of Scripture in a number of places in *The Christian Faith*, and by means of it seeks to establish a unique place for the New Testament as a substitute for the concept of revealed propositional truth which he has discarded.

Thus, Schleiermacher accepted the general view of the Enlightenment—that Christianity was older than the New Testament—but the form of this acceptance was not the deistic position that true Christianity was human reason (which had existed since creation), but the more restricted position that Christianity stemmed from Christ, and that none of the New Testament was written until several years after his death. Thus, Schleiermacher's general position with respect to the Bible rests on an inheritance from the Enlightenment. The Bible is to be regarded as a human production rather than as an emanation from God; it is a manmade book rather than the speech of God; the authors of the Bible were men writing under the influence of the Holy Spirit; the author of the Bible is not God (in the sense that God wrote propositions of human speech).

Some of Schleiermacher's more particular principles with respect to the Bible are also to be traced to the Enlightenment. One of the most important effects of rationalism on Christianity is the development of biblical criticism. At the time of the Reformation, critical methods, both theological and literary, had been used in the examination of the biblical text, but this had been largely suppressed under the influence of scholastic orthodoxy. It received fresh impetus during the time of the Enlightenment and has continued to have an influence long after the Enlightenment came to an end as a recognizable movement. The more moderate wing of biblical critics had an important influence on Schleiermacher's understanding of the Bible. Semler, the outstanding critical scholar at the end of the eighteenth century, was teaching at Halle during Schleiermacher's student days.[13] One of his leading principles was the denial of the equal value of the Old and New Testaments. This was another form of the rationalistic attack upon the received doctrine of inspiration, and Semler advocated a distinction between Scripture and the word of God. He also pointed out the different types of theology represented by the various authors of the New Testament, and investigated the textual inaccuracies of the received text.

Schleiermacher adopted many of Semler's opinions, notably that about the differing value of the two Testaments. Like Semler, he objected to the

---

12. *Christian Faith*, vol. 2 (131:1), 604–5.
13. Galling, *Die Religion in Geschichte und Gegenwart*, vol. 5, 1695–96

practice of lifting verses out of their context to use as proofs for doctrinal propositions. However, he set a higher value on the unity of the New Testament than Semler did. For Schleiermacher, each individual author in the New Testament had his own personal character, which was the basis of his own personal witness to Christ. But behind the varied accounts there is a real unity, which is the Holy Spirit, the common influence derived from the life of Christ. Just as an individual character is to be found in the writings of any author, which is most truly grasped from a total impression of all of said author's writings, so is there a particular spirit discernible from a total impression of the gathered works of the New Testament. This is the Holy Spirit, whose work is the faithful preservation of the apostolic writings and who also works in the church of the present day to enable us to recognize the authoritative nature of the New Testament—and furthermore to distinguish difficult matters within the New Testament.

The central position of Christ in the New Testament was the concept which caused Schleiermacher to reject one of the major emphases of the Enlightenment. Many authors regarded the positive value of Christianity as resting on the inculcation of moral principle. Kant, although his critique of the principles of epistemology represented the end of the Enlightenment, nevertheless represented the position of the rationalists in his moral teaching. He asserted that religion was the recognition of one's duty as the command of God.[14] Duty is the same thing as the categorical imperative by which we act, not in response to any natural interest but because as rational and responsible people we recognize a law which is more important than any particular interest. Natural religion is to know our duty and recognize it as the will of God. Christianity is the perfect natural religion because it inculcates love toward God, and love toward our fellow men. This is the same thing as the categorical imperative: duty for the sake of duty.

In such a presentation the central idea of the New Testament is that of setting forth human duty and giving strong impetus to its observance. Schleiermacher did not accept this position. Religion is not to be found in revealed truth or in moral duty; it is the concern of self-conscious feeling. Schleiermacher gave a very high value to ethics in his presentation of Christianity. Ethics is a presupposition of dogmatics, and moral obedience is a more important aspect of Christian life than knowledge of dogmatic teaching. But for Schleiermacher, duty is not the link between God and humanity; law does not represent the will of God; moral imperatives are not the proper approach to the service of God. Instead, Christianity is based on the

---

14. One of Kant's late works was *Religion innerhalb der Grenzen der blossen Vernunft* (Koenigsberg, 1793). M'Giffert characterizes this as a forceful and lofty statement of eighteenth-century deism. See M'Giffert, *Protestant Thought Before Kant*, 249–50.

feeling of absolute dependence. The perfect example of this feeling is found in Christ, and its influence on us is through the Holy Spirit, whose work we recognize in the Scriptures. Thus, Schleiermacher rejects the interpretation of the Bible that would make moral law its central conception. The center of the New Testament is Christ, and the work of Christ is carried on by the Christian community as the locus of the work of the Holy Spirit. In this respect, Schleiermacher worked out his theology as a reaction to the ideas of the Enlightenment. At many points in his thought, it is possible to trace his ambivalent attitude toward rationalism. In some respects, his theology is built upon basic concepts of Enlightenment philosophy, whereas in others, the relationship is one of contrast and rejection. His relationship with the Enlightenment is thus very similar to his relationship with pietism. His approach to the Bible rested on pietism and the Enlightenment, but his system was frequently a reaction against both.

SCHOLASTIC ORTHODOXY

With respect to a third type of Protestant thought from his day, Schleiermacher's relationship was more straightforward. Official orthodoxy was consistently rejected throughout his system, particularly with respect to the doctrine of the Bible. A major reason for this was the obstacle which strict conformity to confessional statements placed in the way of biblical criticism. In his article "On the Characteristic Value and Binding Aspect of Symbolic Books," Schleiermacher strongly objects to the use of the Protestant confessions as exact standards to which all teaching and preaching within the church must conform:

> What is best and most essential in our theology is the noble form which dogmatics assumed at the Reformation, and the active impulse which was then received towards the study of the Scriptures and concerning the Scriptures. Our asset in this matter is beyond challenge, for when even the Roman Church has adopted it in part, it has done so in large measure through the effect of Protestantism upon it.... But what would become of this asset if a strong and powerfully enforced obligation to the symbolic books should become general? At first, unquestionably, the speculative and the historical spirit would strain and struggle against it, and would seek by all means to do what was possible to make the spirit of the symbolic books prevail over the letter. But in the end, the more the majority made chains for itself, the less would questions arise out of free investigation and disposition, so that both would tend to disappear from our

seats of learning and from our world of books. This would apply not only to dogmatics, but even more to biblical exposition; for interest in the latter will soon cease, if it is not permitted any influence. If everything which appears in the symbolic books is hallowed in equal measure; if the biblical representation of the last judgement is made a dogma in precisely the same sense as the doctrine of the Son of God, and the magical effects of the devil upon the soul in the same sense as the effect of the divine Spirit through the Word: then on remaining matters nothing remains which is worthy of the care of the exegete. Of the scientific form, if it is maintained, nothing would remain but scholastic exactitude in dogmatics, grammatical and lexicographical perfection in exegesis. At the end nothing would remain of theology except an area purely traditional, separated from the rest of education, and thus it would die out.[15]

In this article, Schleiermacher expresses his conviction about the necessary connection between theology and general intellectual life. Any attempt to separate the two he regarded as mistaken and dangerous to both sides. The use of the Bible within the church is twofold: it builds up personal faith, and it provides the people with a means whereby they may judge acutely between what is praiseworthy and what is perverted within the church. But such a judgment must be made in accordance with the spirit and not the letter of the Bible. It rests upon a free disposition and an inner certainty which has nothing to do with an outward, formal, written standard. The effect of such a personal Christian freedom will be to draw together the members of the church in closer fellowship, not so that they may draw clever distinctions between what is correct belief and what is false, but so that they may be free to express their community of spirit and thus to demonstrate their faith in their lives.

Schleiermacher retains the creeds and confessions of the church as important sources of teaching. In particular the Reformation confessions are the marks of a fresh starting point in the history of Christianity, and any system of theology must be loyal to their spirit if it wishes to be considered Protestant in character. Their primary objective is to define the difference between Roman Catholicism as the old form of faith, and Protestantism as the new form. In particular, their definitions of the doctrines of justification and good works, the church and the power of the church, the mass, the ministry of the saints, and religious vows are considered great achievements which must be maintained in all new forms of Protestant teaching.[16] For this

---

15. *Saemmtliche Werke*, part I, vol. 5 (*Symbolischer Buecher*), 441.
16. *Symbolischer Buecher*, 451.

reason, he urges the retention of those confessions which are definitive of Protestantism—such as the Augsburg Confession and the Heidelberg Catechism—but not those which represent scholastic orthodoxy—such as the Formula of Concord and the decrees of the Synod of Dort. In his attitude to the Bible and to the confessions, Schleiermacher represents the type of Protestant thought which stressed the contrast of the spirit and the letter, rather than that which emphasized correctness of doctrine. His polemic is frequently directed against the correctness of orthodoxy. The aim of teaching must not be formal correctness, but a presentation which may be used in the practical teaching of congregations for the strengthening of faith:

> The definitions of the Schools have long since become a dead letter in which no one any longer can find refuge. For the devotional phraseology even of the most orthodox teachers, in so far as they are not content simply to hand on the letter of tradition but aim at edification and confirmation in a living faith, is so remote from the terminology of the schools that it would hardly be possible to find any current terms to bridge the gulf.[17]

His own system of doctrine is formulated to run counter to scholasticism, both prior and subsequent to the Reformation. His interpretation of the Bible is conceived in the same way. The Bible should be used for the edification of the people, and also to make them alert to the Christian spirit and sensitive to what is constructive or perverted in dogmatic teaching. Teaching from the Bible should be directed toward producing a disposition which expresses the needs and the inner certainty of faith: "Such a use of Scripture will never produce an understanding which confines itself to judging the letter of doctrine."[18] Thus, Schleiermacher, while holding the confessions of the Protestant churches in an honorable place in his thought, rejected any thought that they should be decisive for biblical interpretation. In a later chapter in the present study, further consideration will be given to the influence of the teaching of the church on interpretation.[19] Meanwhile, it may be observed that this influence, for Schleiermacher, could never be accorded the position of binding legislation.

---

17. *Christian Faith*, vol. 2 (96:2), 396.
18. *Symbolischer Buecher*, 438.
19. See ch. 6.

2

The Psychological Starting Point

IN THE PREFACE TO his first *Critique*, Kant compared his procedure in philosophy with that of Copernicus's in astronomy. Copernicus had set the sun in the center of the heavenly bodies and said that the earth revolved around it. Kant, instead of making intuition conform to the constitution of objects, made objects conform to the constitution of our faculty of intuition. The result was the start of a new period in philosophical thinking, so that modern philosophy may be divided between pre-Kantian and post-Kantian thought. In a similar way, a division in Protestant thought is marked by the writings of Schleiermacher. Prior to Schleiermacher, theology was regarded as the exposition of a known body of truth deduced from infallible propositions. After Schleiermacher, the center of attention was focused on general religious history, and the nature and varieties of religious experience. Schleiermacher is thus the herald of a new era in Christian thought, one whose message is full of implications for present-day theology. His theological principles are still the center of intense discussion. His specific formulations of doctrine have been consistently rejected, but his general approach has become characteristic of a great deal of Protestant thought.

As Barth writes, his influence is to be found among many who disavow him: "Nobody can say today whether we have really overcome his influence, or whether we are still at heart children of his age for all the protest against him."[1] Central to the revolution in theological thinking are the general

1. Barth, *From Rousseau to Ritschl*, 307.

concepts applicable to the interpretation of the Bible. Prior to Schleiermacher, the Bible was regarded, in orthodox circles, as a body of revealed truth whose individual propositions each contain the words of God. After Schleiermacher came the great development of the history of religions, in which human history was regarded as an advance from the primitive to the civilized, with religious development proceeding in harmony with the general development of humankind. The Bible was just one document representative of this progress. The Old and New Testaments illustrate the change from the primitive to the more sophisticated, but neither one is really unique, nor has either one an indispensable place in the relationship of man to God. Schleiermacher did not truly represent either the orthodox or the "history of religions" approach, but his assertion of the human authorship of the Bible was a large step in the direction of modern relativism. The contrast between Schleiermacher and the thought of preceding centuries may be seen by comparing some of his statements with the following section of one of Calvin's prefaces to his *Institutes*:

> Although the Holy Scriptures contain a perfect doctrine, to which nothing can be added—our Lord having been pleased therein to unfold the infinite treasures of his wisdom—still every person, not intimately acquainted with them, stands in need of some guidance and direction, as to what he ought to look for in them, that he may not wander up and down, but pursue a certain path, and so attain the end to which the Holy Spirit invites him.
>
> And since we are bound to acknowledge that all truth and sound doctrine proceed from God, I will venture boldly to declare what I think of this work, acknowledging it to be God's work rather than mine. To him, indeed, the praise due to it must be ascribed. My opinion of the work then is this: I would exhort all who reverence the word of the Lord, to read it, if they would, in the first place, have a summary of Christian doctrine, and, in the second place, an introduction to the profitable reading both of the Old and New Testament.[2]

Instead of a deposit of perfect doctrine, Schleiermacher calls the Scriptures "only one special instance of the witness to Christ."[3] Instead of requiring learned guidance for the proper approach to Scripture, every Christian

---

2. Calvin, preface to the French edition of 1545, *Institutes of the Christian Religion*, 22–23.

3. Schleiermacher, *Christian Faith*, vol. 2 (127:2), 588.

is free to interpret—provided he sets out from the words of the Redeemer, and from faith in him:

> The fact that the interpretation of the Bible itself is often contentious ought not to be the source of any new human opinion to the effect that one person or another alone knew how to interpret it. We ought not to forestall the Spirit of God, or set limits and goals for him, but rather consider the word of the apostle: "If, however, one thinks differently, God will also reveal it to him." (Phil. 3:15)[4]

Instead of asserting that doctrine comes from God, Schleiermacher said that Christian doctrines are "nothing but the expressions given to the Christian self-consciousness and its connexions."[5] Instead of dogmatics being a summary of divine doctrine and an introduction to the Bible, Schleiermacher regarded it as "the science which systematizes the doctrine prevalent in a Christian Church at a given time."[6]

Schleiermacher's revolutionary approach to the Bible rested on his concept of language as the fundamental means of communication. All language is human communication, in its broadest form, including all sorts of gesture and symbolism, but in its more developed form is concentrated more directly in speech, whether of a spoken or a written kind. Speech is a human phenomenon and it cannot give expression to the being of God as he is in himself. This is Schleiermacher's form of the proposition that what is finite is incapable of bearing what is infinite:

> If one faith wishes to establish the validity of its own application of the idea as against others, it cannot at all accomplish this by the assertion that its own divine communication is pure and entire truth, while the others contain falsehood. For complete truth would mean that God made Himself known as He is in and for Himself. But such a truth could not proceed outwardly from any fact, and even if it did in some incomprehensible way come to a human soul, it could not be apprehended by that soul, and retained as a thought; and if it could not be in any way perceived and retained, it could not become operative. Any proclamation of God which is to be operative upon and within us can only express God in his relation to us; and this is not an

---

4. *Saemmtliche Werke*, part II, vol. 2 (*Vierte-Siebente Sammlung*), 632
5. *Christian Faith*, vol. 1 (13), 66.
6. *Christian Faith*, vol. 1 (19), 88.

infra-human ignorance concerning God, but the essence of human limitedness in relation to Him.[7]

Hence, revelation cannot be propositions; revelation is the appearance of something absolutely new by which God begins a new act of creation. Any propositions about this revelation are human propositions seeking to communicate it to others. All that exists is the effect of an act or decree of God; we cannot speak of the act or decree itself, but only of the effect as it appears to us. The whole world is under the governance of God, but we have no means by which to conceptualize this: "It is therefore only within the compass of our own world that the divine government is known to us—within the sphere, that is, in which redemption makes its power felt."[8]

It is within this framework that the Bible is to be seen. The Bible is human communication; its function is to proclaim God in a way which may be operative among men; its message of Christ is the highest expression of God as he is in relation to us. Thus, the Bible is not without error; it contains matter which is incidental to the gospel and whose inclusion is the result of local circumstances in the early church. Schleiermacher wishes to make the sharpest possible distinction between God and the world: the Bible, as an instance of human language, belongs on the worldly side of the division.

This concept of language determined for Schleiermacher the starting point for theology. Calvin had stated that doctrine included knowledge of God and knowledge of the human, and that it was difficult to know which should be accorded temporal priority. He concluded that "due arrangement" required treatment first of the knowledge of God.[9] Schleiermacher reversed the procedure: because all doctrine was human speech, it is necessary first to consider the status of human communication and the structure of the human person before we consider how God's acts are to be seen in relation to us. Locating the starting point with humanity was not in itself a new departure for Protestant theology. It had been an accepted approach for instructional manuals from the early period of the Reformation. Thus, Luther's exposition of the creed in the Smaller Catechism deals with creation as the creation of the individual. Similarly, Calvin's *Geneva Catechism* begins with the question of the purpose of human life. Schleiermacher's new departure was to assert the human starting point as an integral part of dogmatic procedure. The starting point of his theology is also the starting point for his interpretation of the Bible.

---

7. *Christian Faith*, vol. 1 (10), 52.
8. *Christian Faith*, vol. 2 (164:2), 724.
9. Calvin, *Institutes*, vol. 1, 1.

Schleiermacher's starting point in humanity was centered in human self-consciousness. In developing his concept of self-consciousness, the influence of pietism and critical philosophy had combined. Both had denied that religion is to be truly expressed in dogmatic statements of a metaphysical type. Pietism had rejected German orthodox Protestantism's tradition of outlining correct teaching in confessional statements. "Feeling" is the word which expresses the characteristic approach of pietism, and feeling became the central concept in Schleiermacher's treatment of religious self-consciousness. The critical philosophy of Kant had demonstrated the impossibility of metaphysical knowledge: speculation of a metaphysical sort could prove nothing which was of value to religion one way or another. For Kant, the solution to the problem of knowledge was to be found in categories of apperception, which regulate all possible experience. Experience and knowledge were thus considered as aspects of the human person, and the attention of philosophy was centered on problems of self-consciousness. Dilthey regarded the emphasis on the self-consciousness as Schleiermacher's principal debt to Kant.[10] For Kant, self-consciousness is the basis of the validation of knowledge; for Schleiermacher, self-consciousness is the locus of religion—and feeling, as an aspect of self-consciousness, is a unique source of piety. Self-consciousness is the aspect of human nature which provides the starting point for theology.

The concept of self-consciousness became, for Schleiermacher, the key to the understanding of John 1:14, which in turn was one of the passages of the Bible which he regarded as central to the whole enterprise of theology. In one of his letters to Dr. Luecke concerning *The Christian Faith*, he said that he wished he could make more evident the fact that his whole dogmatic should be considered as based upon this text.[11] In that work itself he speaks of the God-consciousness of Christ as the continual living presence of God in Christ, and bases it upon the phrase "the Word became flesh": "for 'Word' is the activity of God expressed in the form of consciousness, and 'flesh' is a general expression for the organic."[12] Consciousness is the special gift of God to men, which in the purely natural state they have perverted into all kinds of unrighteousness. In Christ, the Word of God has become flesh so that we might receive him, for something can only apprehend what is similar to itself. Thus, it was necessary for Christ to become a man in every sense, like other men, except for sin, in order to communicate with us. Some other appearance of God would have overpowered us, but could

---

10. Dilthey, *Leben Schleiermachers*, 94.
11. *Saemmtliche Werke*, part I, vol. 2 (*Luecke*), 611.
12. *Christian Faith*, vol. 2 (96:3), 397.

not have made any conscious impression upon us.[13] Hence the self-consciousness of Christ is of vital importance for theology; it is the perfected God-consciousness, which acknowledges in each moment that everything that exists is absolutely dependent upon God. In Christ, there is a new implanting of the God-consciousness in human nature, which creates the possibility of new religious self-consciousness in humankind.[14] This new self-consciousness is the aspect of the new humanity which makes it proper to begin theology with the conception of humanity. Schleiermacher's conception of self-consciousness has been the center of the critical discussion of his theology. In order to evaluate its position in his biblical interpretation, we must examine its development in *The Christian Faith*, and also see what some commentators have made of it. *The Christian Faith* has been called the first great sustained definition of Christian belief since the Reformation. In it, Schleiermacher developed his ideas of religion as a human phenomenon, with its starting point in the psychological constitution of human personality rather than in the transcendent God.

PSYCHOLOGY IN THE CHRISTIAN FAITH

Schleiermacher's famous definition of God is found in the fourth section of *The Christian Faith*: "The *Whence* of our receptive and active existence . . . is to be designated by the word 'God,' and . . . this is for us the really original signification of that word."[15]

This definition is one of several remarkable statements in the opening section of that work which mark its originality, and have been the center of heated argument in theological circles ever since. The whole of *The Christian Faith* consists of working out these initial concepts. The idea of God is psychologically based: God is the source of human existence in the active or passive states of human self-consciousness.

Schleiermacher advocated a "faculty psychology," that is, a psychological theory which considered the various faculties or aspects of human personality as constitutive of that personality. In his view, the forms of self-consciousness may be listed as knowing, doing, and feeling, and these three are adequate to describe all human states.[16] The personality does not

---

13. *Saemmtliche Werke*, part II, vol. 8 (*Johannes*), 34, 12; *Saemmtliche Werke*, part II, vol. 3 (*Predigten*), 331.
14. *Christian Faith*, vol. 2 (134:3), 617.
15. *Christian Faith*, vol. 1 (4:4), 16 (italics original).
16. *Christian Faith*, vol. 1 (3), 5; (3:2) 6–7; (3:3) 7–8; (3:4) 8–11.

consist in any one of them alone, but in the three taken together in the total content of life.

Knowing and feeling may be regarded as receptive states, because in them we abide within ourselves, while doing is called an active state, because in it we pass beyond ourselves. Life is to be conceived of as an alternation between a state of abiding-in-self and a state of passing-beyond-self. God is then the source of these states of self-consciousness, and is related equally to the three human aspects of knowing, doing, and feeling.

Religion, however, is concerned only with feeling. Religion is piety, and piety has always been related in common speech to feeling. Schleiermacher considered the essence of a thing to be whatever constituted the measure of the thing's effectiveness. Piety could not be knowledge, because an increase of knowledge did not necessarily mean an increase in effective piety. For the same reason, piety could not be activity. By separating religion from knowledge and action, Schleiermacher was rejecting the religious claims of scholastic orthodoxy and rationalistic moralism. For Schleiermacher, religion is no more to be found in moral action than in dogmatic assertion. Religion is feeling in the immediate self-consciousness, and thus has to do with self-awareness and spontaneity. It is not an affair of the subconscious, nor is it the result of self-contemplation. By linking religion to feeling, Schleiermacher sought a way to do justice to faith, while at the same time leaving scientific investigation perfectly free to pursue its own course without conflict from religion. In particular he was concerned about historical inquiry, rather than natural science, but ever since his years among the Moravians he had objected to any use of dogmatic statements which might hinder free inquiry. In his own case, the necessary free investigation involved the historical authenticity of ancient literary documents, both of classical and biblical literature. In order to provide the necessary scientific freedom, he dissolved the connection between faith and facts. Christian belief does not consist in asserting certain things to be facts, but in an awareness of feeling. Schleiermacher sought in this way to avoid the clash of theology and science by avoiding the twin dangers—on the one hand, of a scientific view which seeks to reduce God to an object of scientific investigation, and on the other hand, of a theology which presumes to establish facts and validate theories which may be used in science. Schleiermacher sought to find a middle ground which would establish the proper province of each discipline and prevent encroachment of the one upon the other.

The feeling which is the basis of every religion is the feeling of absolute dependence.[17] In Schleiermacher's view, this feeling is the same thing as the

---

17. *Christian Faith*, vol. 1 (4), 12; (4:1) 12–13; (4:2) 13–15; (4:3) 15–16; (4:4) 16–18.

consciousness of being in relation to God. The active and receptive states of self-consciousness may be designated as self-caused and nonself-caused elements of personality. With respect to what is self-caused, we have a feeling of freedom; with respect to what is nonself-caused, we have a feeling of dependence. Towards most things, we have an alternating sense: in some respects, we have a feeling of freedom, because by our action we can, in principle at least, affect what a thing is and what it does; in other respects, we have a feeling of dependence because the thing is there and by it our action and our own being are determined. The feeling of freedom is never absolute, because we always have a sense of the limitation of our own activity; but the feeling of dependence is absolute, because we have the sense that all of our activity is finally based on a source outside of ourselves. This source is God, and the feeling is the feeling of absolute dependence.

God is differentiated from the world, because toward the world we have at least a partial feeling of freedom. We are active in the world, and our activity has an effect upon the world. Our influence upon the world is not large, and to a great extent our feeling toward the world is one of dependence. But our dependence upon the world is not absolute. The only source for the feeling of absolute dependence is God, and toward God both the world and we ourselves are totally dependent. God is thus designated as completely separated from humanity and the world. God is complete otherness, neither part of the world, nor to be seen in part or all of the world. He can neither be affected by human action, nor grasped by human thought; he is not an object of knowledge. Like Kant, Schleiermacher denied the speculative approach to God and rejected metaphysical knowledge of God. Whereas Kant bridged the gap between the human and God by means of moral principles, Schleiermacher maintained that the point of their contact was the self-consciousness newly created in Jesus Christ.

The work of dogmatic theology, in Schleiermacher's view, is to systematize doctrine—and normally it would include three types of propositions: descriptions of human states, explanations of the properties and actions of God, and statements about the constitution of the world.[18] In accordance with his psychological criterion, Schleiermacher admits only the first type of proposition as proper to dogmatics. Thus, all statements about God must be capable of being expressed in terms of statements about human states of mind. The feeling of absolute dependence is itself the presence of God in the self-consciousness, and so all divine attributes can be formulated in such a way that they refer to self-consciousness. Dogmatic language being what it is, it is not possible to do away altogether with statements about God and

18. *Christian Faith*, vol. 1 (30), 125; (30:2) 126.

about the world, but all legitimate statements must be able to bear a psychological form. As a result, Schleiermacher does not discuss the doctrine of God in a single series of connected passages, but divides the material according to various aspects of self-consciousness:

> All attributes which we ascribe to God are to be taken as denoting not something special in God, but only something special in the manner in which the feeling of absolute dependence is to be related to him.[19]

The aim of Schleiermacher's discussion of the attributes of God is to limit all expressions which imply an analogy between God and finite being. Traditional discussions of the divine nature have always included speculative material which is directed toward a philosophical rather than a religious interest.

Schleiermacher's discussion of the doctrine of God seeks to serve only a religious interest, not pretending to outline a complete knowledge of God, but ensuring that the various expressions of the God-consciousness are included in it. The attributes of God are dealt with in *The Christian Faith* on the basis of the general division which is made among the various aspects of religious self-consciousness. The first section considers those aspects of self-consciousness referring to the general relationship between God and the world. In it, Schleiermacher considers the attributes of eternity, omnipresence, omnipotence, and omniscience. In the second and third sections, he develops his discussion of the religious self-consciousness as it concerns redemption. All sense of alienation from God is expressed as the consciousness of sin, in connection with which the attributes of holiness and justice arise; all sense of fellowship with God comes from the consciousness of grace, and the attributes of love and wisdom are then relevant. The divine attributes do not refer to a multiplicity of functions, separate from each other and opposed to one another in certain particulars. The difference between one attribute and another is not a difference within God, but only a difference within the religious self-consciousness—and each attribute in its own way expresses the whole being of God.

One of these attributes can be considered here as a demonstration of the method. The holiness of God is one of the attributes which is connected with the consciousness of sin.[20] Holiness in God corresponds to the con-

---

19. *Christian Faith*, vol. 1 (50), 194.

20. *Christian Faith*, vol. 1 (83), 341; (83:1), 341–42. In his discussion of the holiness of God, Schleiermacher cites only one text: 1 Peter 1:14–16. He remarks: "[T]he holiness of God is associated with the demand that we should no longer live according to our lusts in ignorance." No acknowledgment is made of the quotation from the Old

science of man, which is part of our consciousness of the need of redemption. In particular, conscience refers to that aspect of the self-consciousness, which results in activity. Our consciousness of God confronts us with moral demands, and it is deviation from these demands which arouses in us a sense of hindrance of life, which is the sense of sin. Conscience can never express the whole of our God-consciousness, because it implies a discrepancy between our understanding and our will, a discrepancy that is the source of our actions' deviation from the moral standard. But conscience is an aspect of our sense of dependence upon God, and as such is thought of as the voice of God within us, an original revelation of God. The discrepancy which we find between our awareness of God as holy and the awareness of him as love is not a division within God, but only in our self-consciousness. Sin and redemption are antinomies of human existence, but they have their source in the one consciousness of God, which underlies all human states.

In all this discussion, Schleiermacher is seeking to avoid any speculative projection of the idea of God beyond the conceptions of human consciousness. Systems of speculative ideas can be constructed which include theoretical propositions about God. But these speculations are useless for religious purposes. Religion, for Schleiermacher, is a practical matter of human life, and dogmatic theology as the systematization of religious propositions must serve the purposes of practical piety. The only function of the concept of the holiness of God is that it places a claim upon religious self-consciousness in its active aspect in the form of a moral demand. As a theoretical projection about the being of God, it has no value for piety and results only in an inconsistent and disruptive conception. In a similar way, Schleiermacher discusses the various attributes of God from the point of view of their significance for the religious self-consciousness. Various materials from traditional theology are discussed in categories which are derived from the concept of self-consciousness, and they are retained, altered, or rejected on the basis of their agreement with the psychological categories. Schleiermacher's approach is empirical and his statements are derived, as much as possible, from religious experience. Religion is an important aspect of human life which cannot be adequately dealt with by categories applicable to knowledge or action, and although it is connected in many ways with other aspects of human life, it does not need any support from them in establishing its own existence and validity.

Testament in verse 16.

MODIFICATION OF THE PSYCHOLOGICAL APPROACH

Despite the clarity with which Schleiermacher sets out the psychological starting point of his thought, it is a matter of no little difficulty to judge its real importance in his system. Some commentators consider that it is the central theme of his thought, to be used to interpret all he wrote, no matter how different in tone other passages may be. Paul Loeffler, in his article "Self-Consciousness and Self-Understanding as Theological Principles in Schleiermacher and Bultmann,"[21] speaks of the derivation of the feeling of absolute dependence from the immediate self-consciousness as the decisive procedure which determines Schleiermacher's whole theology. Loeffler's interpretation is that we cannot have any comprehension of God apart from the self-consciousness, except in a symbolic manner which reflects the self-consciousness, and there can be no objective acts of God which faith may acknowledge. Among the consequences which Loeffler draws from this is that the possibility of revelation is confined to the self-consciousness, and that there can be no objective word from God given in history. Therefore the Bible becomes a secondary document—just one form of expression of the pious self-consciousness. God can no longer speak directly to man in the Bible. Furthermore, the acts of God pertain only to the realm of human self-consciousness, and thus the structure of the human self becomes an unbreakable framework for all theological thought.

Loeffler's interpretation raises questions which will be more fully dealt with in the chapters which follow, but here they will be considered briefly in order to establish the proper significance of Schleiermacher's so-called "psychologism." In the first place, Schleiermacher's use of the word *revelation* is equivocal. It does not exhaust his meaning to say that the possibility of revelation is confined to the self-consciousness. Speaking of the divine revelation in Christ and the possibility of human nature taking the divine into itself, Schleiermacher says that this *possibility* must be completed by an actual implanting which is *"purely a divine act."*[22] Schleiermacher is referring to the incarnation, and the act in question is also "an action of human nature." Precisely at this point, Schleiermacher admits that he is at the boundary of the "universal spiritual life," and that therefore it is impossible to express truly what is meant by this divine action, which is also a human action. However, the human possibility and human action are nothing without the divine act. The term *revelation* is used variously by Schleiermacher to refer to a fact and to a conception. A fact is something given; it is perceived in experience,

---

21. Loeffler, "Selbstbewusstsein und Selbstverstaendnis," 304–15.
22. *Christian Faith*, vol. 1 (13:1), 64 (italics mine).

and hence suprarational. A conception is something conceived in the mind and transmitted by speech, and hence it is purely rational. Schleiermacher says, "Between the rational and the suprarational, there can be no connexion."²³ For Schleiermacher, sometimes revelation is "the originality of the fact" which lies at the basis of Christianity; sometimes revelation is an idea which arises in the soul. Schleiermacher denies that revelation is essentially doctrine. Doctrine is implied by revelation, but such doctrine rests on the impression made upon us of a distinctive existence. The basis of all revelation is an original fact, and it is only the original working of that fact which is confined to the self-consciousness. The principle is the one which we have already seen: God's being and God's acts in themselves are beyond human capacity to conceive or to communicate; only as they work upon, or impress, or affect our human self-consciousness can they be apprehended or spoken of. All propositions about revelation therefore relate to the human self-consciousness, but revelation itself is not merely a matter of the human self-consciousness: it depends on an act of God in history.

Several instances of this double aspect of revelation will be seen in the pages which follow. First and essentially, the act of God is seen in Jesus Christ. In him is seen God's new work of creation; he is the original fact of Christianity; he is the given of revelation, in comparison with whom "everything which could otherwise be regarded as revelation again loses this character"²⁴; his originality is the existence of God in him, which creates the new humanity. The life of Christ is historical fact reported in the Gospels, which, at least in part, represent eyewitness reports of events which happened and were objectively perceived. In particular, the resurrection was a fact in that in the days after the crucifixion, Jesus was seen and heard and touched by many of his closest followers. The raising of Lazarus was also a fact, perceived not only by Jesus' friends, but also by his enemies. These things are acts of God in the realm of perceptible reality, but they can only be recognized as such by the human self-consciousness because of the receptivity for spiritual discernment created by Christ. Thus, many saw the raising of Lazarus, but only a few understood it as the act of God in Christ. It is Christ himself, in Schleiermacher's view, who is the Word of God in history, and the gospel accounts of his life are thoroughly objective accounts of what he said and did. The communication of this word is through the transmission of the original self-proclamation of Christ, and the Bible is the record of this self-proclamation and the witness to the word. God speaks directly to man in the original proclamation.

23. *Christian Faith*, vol. 1 (13), 66; see also (10) 47–52.
24. *Christian Faith*, vol. 1 (13:1), 63; see also vol. 2 (94:3), 388–89.

Schleiermacher's concept of the special acts of God in history is best seen in the person of Jesus Christ, but it is not confined to him. Another instance, closely related to it, is seen in Schleiermacher's doctrine of the Lord's Supper. The effectiveness of the sacrament, in which Christ is present, "flows directly from the Word of institution."[25] As will be noted below, the institution of the communion is traced back to the supper which Christ himself held with his disciples, and the words of institution are the words which he spoke. If the charge of psychologism made against Schleiermacher were really adequate, it would need to be relevant to his teaching on communion. Here, if anywhere, there has been a tendency within Protestantism to see the acts of God as dependent upon and bound to the self-consciousness of the believer. Precisely here, in Schleiermacher's position, this tendency is not present. The efficacy of the sacrament is independent both of the officiating minister and of "any special and inward spontaneity" on the part of the receivers. In this connection, it is worthy of note that Schleiermacher's last act was the celebration of communion. Virtually his last words were in reference to the words of institution: "On these words of the Scripture I rely, they are the foundation of my faith."[26]

In the light of these considerations, the following comments may be made on Loeffler's propositions. We cannot have any comprehension of God apart from the self-consciousness, because comprehension itself is a self-conscious activity; apart from self-consciousness, the word "comprehension" has no meaning, but this does not make God either a projection of self-consciousness or a symbolic representation. For Schleiermacher, there are acts of God which faith may acknowledge. Everything that exists is the effect of the act of God, and to the eye of faith, each thing may be seen as such; this is what God-consciousness means. But, in addition, there are special effects of God's act in Jesus Christ—such as the resurrection, the raising of Lazarus, and the sacrament of the Lord's Supper. If we do not speak of the acts of God in themselves, it is not because God does not act, but because we can only see and comprehend and use words to designate the *effects* of the action of God. Revelation is communication, is both objective act of God and subjective impression upon the self-consciousness of humanity. If the Bible has become secondary in this system, it is secondary only to Christ and to faith. Schleiermacher can conceive of a situation in which the Bible is destroyed without faith being destroyed, but it still remains the norm for all expressions of faith. Thus, while the Bible is secondary to Christ, it remains the primary document of faith.

25. *Christian Faith*, vol. 2 (139:2), 640–41.
26. *Aus Schleiermachers Leben in Briefen*, vol. 2, 339.

SUMMARY

Schleiermacher's concept of self-consciousness may be summarized by referring to some passages from his sermons. The God-consciousness known to Christian faith is newly implanted in humanity with the coming of Jesus. His self-consciousness, which is absolutely powerful, is the ideal human self-consciousness which we approach as we come nearer to him. For Christ, the God-consciousness was the center of his whole being and the determinant of all his action. In a sermon on John 14:27, Schleiermacher uses the concept of God-consciousness to explain what "peace" means for Christ:

> What was the Redeemer's peace? It was this: that he was completely one with his Father for ever, in every relationship: that the eye of his spirit never opened itself to look at something near him without seeing it as a work of God; that no stimulus in his soul developed itself into a determination of his will without his having perceived, in what was incumbent upon him, the will of God on the matter. Christ and his Father assumed one another in such a way that Christ recognized the works of his Father, and the Father always showed him greater works. The Redeemer did his Father's will, and he was always carried forward in this fulfilment of the divine will until he was able to say that he had finished everything.[27]

The unity between God and man in Christ is a conscious unity, which meant that there could be no conflict or opposition between them. In other men, Christ has implanted this consciousness, but it is not fully developed or perfected. The resulting opposition between human will and God's will gives rise to pain, which is the result of sin. Sin is the only human phenomenon not applicable to the Redeemer. He has a great sympathy for the human sinner, but he himself is completely sinless. For other men, assumption into Christ means the development of their God-consciousness so that, more and more, it becomes like his. In an earlier sermon on John 19:30, he had envisaged the religious self-consciousness of a person who was close to the Redeemer in the hour of death:

> He who will praise the grace of the Lord, he who is not deaf to the voice of his Spirit, he who finds himself in such living fellowship with Christ that for Christ and for him all things are common, in the last moment may look back upon such a life which he has lived in faith in the Son of God, and which the Son

---

27. *Saemmtliche Werke*, part II, vol. 3 (*Predigten*), 2.

of God has lived in him. This verse from the Scriptures will be the truest expression of his consciousness, and it expresses the full and complete character of his life. What is not to be found here does not belong to his true character. In the believing feeling that this edifying and sanctifying verse has been fulfilled in him, he will be able to say, "It is finished."[28]

Schleiermacher stresses the subjective side of Christian teaching not in order to derive God from the self-consciousness, but in order that we may become aware of redemption, which is the forming in us of the life of Christ. This is the sense in which Schleiermacher interprets Galatians 2:20 and 4:19. Everything must have its source in the life and teaching of Christ. In one of the *Homilies on John*, Schleiermacher attributes this to the work of the Spirit:

> This is the way of each individual Christian disposition. We can first say of a man that has fully known the Lord when he has turned to him with the full acknowledgment of his soul. It is the general impression of the glory of the only-begotten Son of the Father. It is the general feeling that he is the way, the truth and the life. By his life the individual life is always more and more firmly and deeply grounded; it is set in a clear light; it proceeds in living power. To develop this more and more from the very first beginning of faith and love is the work of the divine Spirit.[29]

For Schleiermacher, the Bible is a human book. Its ideas and the conception of God which we draw from it are expressed in human language. All language has its basis in human self-consciousness, and therefore our expressions about God and the attributes which we ascribe to him are grounded in the human self-consciousness. But we cannot say that the center of gravity of Schleiermacher's thought lies with humanity; to do so would contradict his conception of God-consciousness. A proper God-consciousness would enable us to see each thing as a work of God, and each action which we perform as an act of obedience to the will of God. As the God-consciousness is more and more formed in us, the center of gravity of our thought is shifted from human to God. Thus, Schleiermacher's revolutionary approach to theology has a human starting point but a divine goal, and the Bible in his system, although it is a human work, is a response to the "whence" of all our existence formed through the work of Jesus Christ.

---

28. *Saemmtliche Werke*, part II, vol. 2 (*Vierte-Siebente Sammlung*), 146.
29. *Saemmtliche Werke*, part II, vol. 9 (*Johannes*), 461. On John 14:25–31.

3

Hermeneutics: Theory and Practice

SCHLEIERMACHER OUTLINED HIS PRINCIPLES of interpretation in his lectures on hermeneutics. He first lectured on the subject in 1805, but the published version is based on the outline of the subject which he prepared in 1819, and on student notes of courses which he gave between 1826 and 1833. In them, Schleiermacher makes the claim that the task of interpretation is to understand someone's speech better than its originator himself understood it.[1] This distinctive formulation is a phrase which summarizes his conception, and it is central to the discussion of hermeneutics in philosophy and theology subsequent to his work.

Schleiermacher's approach to hermeneutics in these lectures has a theological aim: to set forth general presuppositions and methods to be used in the interpretation of the Bible for the purposes of dogmatic theology. He does not, however, regard the methods used as applicable only to biblical literature. In general, the Bible is to be approached by the same methods which would be used to interpret any other literary work. Schleiermacher was well acquainted with literary problems. The great task of his early years was the translating and editing of Plato's *Dialogues*, a work undertaken in collaboration with Friedrich Schlegel, but completed by Schleiermacher alone.

Hermeneutics, according to Schleiermacher, is the discipline of understanding correctly another person's speech and writing. The act of

---

1. *Saemmtliche Werke*, part I, vol. 7 (*Hermeneutik*), 32.

understanding is to be seen as the reconstruction of the original creative act which produced the speech or writing in the first place. The interpreter must seek to approach the work to be interpreted from the same point of view, as far as this is possible, as that of the original author. To do so, the interpreter must be conscious of many things which, for the author, were unconscious. If the text is in a foreign language, the interpreter must deliberately pay attention to linguistic rules which the author took for granted, or perhaps even did not know. What is true in this example holds true for interpretation generally: spontaneous expression in speech contains many unconscious modes of thought which must be consciously noted by anyone making an interpretation in a thorough and legitimate manner. In this sense, the interpreter must understand the text better than the author, although he need not have better knowledge of any facts reported. The principle is one with a wide application in philology, but Schleiermacher does not mean it either in a scientific or in a general philosophical sense: the interpreter need not have superior knowledge of the subject matter, nor need he be able to discuss the subject on the basis of principles which apply to wider fields of study.

Schleiermacher regarded hermeneutics and textual criticism as companion disciplines, and lectured on them consecutively. In the introduction to the *Hermeneutics*, he states:

> Hermeneutics and criticism, both philological disciplines, both arts, belong together, since the execution of each presupposes the other. The former is in general the art of understanding correctly the speech of another, especially when it is written down. The latter is the art of judging correctly the authenticity of the writings and passages, and of establishing on the basis of adequate attestation and data.[2]

Textual criticism he regards as a part of historical criticism, and separate from doctrinal considerations.[3] It arises out of differences which are found in the texts of ancient books, such as the Bible or classical Greek literature. The existence of such differences establishes the fact that we do not have these writings in the form in which they originally appeared. Textual criticism seeks to reconstruct the text, as nearly as possible, in the form which it originally had, by judging the differences in the text and retaining those readings which have the best historical attestation. It also judges the authenticity of writings to decide if the person to whose authorship the

---

2. *Saemmtliche Werke*, part I, vol. 7 (*Hermeneutik*), 3.

3. *Saemmtliche Werke*, part I, vol. 7 (*Hermeneutik*), 263. This is the section containing the lectures on criticism.

work is ascribed was really the original writer. Schleiermacher distinguishes criticism from doctrinal considerations, because doctrinal judgments might prejudice the critical inquiry, and because the authorship and date of a composition have no bearing upon the doctrinal significance of its ideas. Doctrinal studies may have some relation to criticism by being able to give evidence of the period within which certain ideas were current, and hence whether they could have occurred in the works of certain authors. But in this sense, doctrinal studies serve a historical purpose, not a systematic one. Criticism of a philological kind is thus a companion study to hermeneutics. Within hermeneutics itself, there is a type of interpretation which is similarly a close study of words and literary construction. Schleiermacher calls it grammatical interpretation, and it has to do with the study of the language in which the writing is composed.[4] It concerns itself with the grammar, vocabulary, and style of a foreign language, with the special meanings of words and patterns of thought which were characteristic of the author and his time. This grammatical interpretation is a necessary part of all literary interpretation, and is particularly important in dealing with the New Testament. Without it, understanding becomes a secondhand affair, subject to distortions which are greater than those which would exist if we could make a direct approach to the speech of the author himself.

As an example, Schleiermacher refers to the word *righteousness* (δικαιοσύνη).[5] To express the status of the new man in Christ, Paul had to select words for the communication of his thought. One method would have been to choose words which were totally new so that they could be carefully defined as he wished. The other method was to use words which were current in Jewish religious speech, and by a new use would give them a new meaning. Paul chose the latter alternative, but as a result it is necessary to distinguish between *righteousness* in the Old Testament, meaning obedience to the law, and in Paul's writings, in which it means the gift of God in Christ which creates faith within us. Schleiermacher regards the word in the Sermon on the Mount as bearing the Old Testament rather than the Pauline meaning. However, Schleiermacher was not content with such grammatical, philological, or historical approaches to interpretation:

> As long as hermeneutics is still treated as an aggregate of individual observations of a general or special nature, no matter how fine and commendable they may be, it does not deserve the name of an art.[6]

4. *Saemmtliche Werke*, part I, vol. 7 (*Hermeneutik*), 41.
5. See *Saemmtliche Werke*, part I, vol. 7 (*Hermeneutik*), 116, 133, 138, 139.
6. *Saemmtliche Werke*, part I, vol. 1 (*Kurze Darstellung*), 56. The translation of this

What has to be understood is not simply the objective signification of the words, but rather the individuality of the person who used the words. Once the scientific task is completed, a further task remains which is personal and creative, seeking the inner logic of the composition which explains not what was said, but why it was said in the way that it was. The method for such work is not the mechanical application of rules, but that of an intuitive art. Schleiermacher's approach to interpretation is thus an "aesthetic" one. In one aspect, thought has to do with factual content, but in another aspect, it is the work of artistic creation. Thought in its aesthetic aspect is free and not bound to any corresponding object or event. Thus, poetry and scientific history are two distinct uses of speech, and neither may be judged according to the principles which are regulative in the other. It was characteristic of Schleiermacher's theory of interpretation that he stressed the artistic approach and considered all linguistic expression as free creative activity grounded in the personality of the author. In this regard, he went so far as to regret the lack of any personal writings by Euclid, which would permit one to understand the subjective element in his geometry.[7]

The boundary between spontaneous artistic expression and the mechanical recording of facts is one which is constantly shifting. We must not be content merely to understand the literal meaning of a text, but need also to read between the lines in order to understand the intention which gave rise to the expression in the first place. This requires that the interpreter have the ability to understand language, both extensively and intensively. Extensive knowledge is the recognition of the meaning of words, using the comparison of texts and usages as a method. Intensive knowledge is the ability to feel the living reality of language and to penetrate "into the core of the language in its relation to thought." Intensive knowledge depends on one's ability to know people individually so that one knows "the genuine

---

sentence is taken from the article "Hermeneutic since Barth," in Robinson and Cobb, *New Hermeneutic*, 19. The German word *Kunstlehre*, translated here as "art," is rendered as "technology" throughout Tice's version. Sections 132 and 265 of *Kurze Darstellung* are relevant to the interpretation of this word.

Dr. Tice refers to Schleiermacher's refusal in *The Christian Faith*, section 9, to call Christianity an aesthetic religion. In Christianity, the natural is subordinated to the moral, and in this sense, religion is ethical rather than aesthetic. In a similar way, hermeneutics is not properly aesthetics, because it is not determined entirely by nature. However, Schleiermacher is at pains both in *Hermeneutik* and *Kurze Darstellung* to distinguish the procedure of interpretation from anything mechanical. Interpretation is an intuition, not a set of rules with mathematical precision. Hence, neither "art" nor "technology" is really satisfactory as a translation: the meaning is somewhere between them. See *Brief Outline on the Study of Theology*, 56–57, 93.

7. *Saemmtliche Werke*, part I, vol. 7 (*Hermeneutik*), 151.

meaning of a man and his distinctive characteristics in relation to the essential idea of the man."[8]

The grasping of true individuality is never a mechanical act, but rather a "divinatory" act by which the life-unity of a person is understood and presented. It is readily seen as the way in which we understand the people with whom we deal in everyday conversation. But it is no less necessary in dealing with an author's written compositions. Literary expression is only a part of a person's life, and every person stands in an infinite number of relationships to persons, objects, and events in the world. As these cannot all be known, it is necessary to select from them those relationships which are truly significant—and to form a judicious picture of his real individuality. A written composition represents one aspect of this individuality, and has its source in some particular event in his or her inner history. The interpreter requires to seek out this event by the fullest possible knowledge of the external circumstances, but also by an intuitive grasp of the individuality which is given expression in the composition. The grammatical mode of interpretation must be complemented by the divinatory mode. Both modes are art, for neither can be made mechanical, but in all cases the divinatory mode is indispensable.

Biblical hermeneutics approaches its task in the same way as interpretation of any other written composition. The interpreter must seek to understand the individuality of the authors of the various books in order to grasp what they are saying, and beyond the individual authors, we must seek the expression of the common spirit present in all of them:

> If we cannot ever fully understand each personal distinctive mark of the New Testament writers, it is still possible to achieve the most important object of the undertaking, namely to grasp ever more completely the common life among them, the being and the spirit of Christ.[9]

Previous interpretation of the Bible had been prevented from advancing its methodology because of the dogmatic assertion of unity, which regarded the books as if the same author had written them all. A psychological-individual approach to the different authors of the New Testament is the more fruitful approach. Both grammatical and psychological arts of interpretation are called for, but both must be kept entirely separate from dogmatics, which must pursue its task by methods appropriate to its own field of study. The task of New Testament hermeneutics has some particular

---

8. *Saemmtliche Werke*, part I, vol. 7 (*Hermeneutik*), 17.
9. *Saemmtliche Werke*, part I, vol. 7 (*Hermeneutik*), 262.

problems which illustrate the divinatory method of interpretation. Apart from the Apocalypse, the books are classified as historical and epistolary. The first four have the common title of gospels, with names of their reputed authors as part of their headings. These headings are not part of the original text, and so we have the work of textual criticism to do before we can properly judge the individuality of the books or of their authors or editors. In this case, it is not only true that hermeneutics and philological criticism belong together, but also that the results of the hermeneutical inquiry may supply material for the judgment of historical questions. The common material of the Gospels is the life of Jesus, and a comparison of the various treatments gives an indication of the particular aim of each. Where one author reports a story which another omits, there are two possible reasons: either he lacked the information which the other possessed, or else he chose to omit it because it did not serve any purpose in his conception of the founding of Christianity. Schleiermacher compares Mark's Gospel with that of John and concludes that Mark omitted the birth stories of Jesus because he did not know them, whereas John left them out because they did not serve his aim of presenting Jesus as the founder of the Christian church.[10]

By further comparison of John and all three Synoptic Gospels with respect to the story of Christ's sufferings in Jerusalem, we can see that the Synoptics recount a series of disconnected incidents, whereas John presents a connected story even though there are some gaps in it.[11] In general, John's Gospel gives a presentation which has a number of time references from which a general chronological sequence can be determined. He does not recount incidents simply for their own sake, but in a connected way which sees them as parts of a whole. Christ is presented as a person with an evident relationship to the national life, and this relationship is presented as he deals with public crowds and with those in authority. His clashes with groups and with individuals are presented as the preparation for the final catastrophe of the cross. This unity of viewpoint in John's Gospel gives us material for a hermeneutical judgment which leads to a solution to the question of historical priority among the Gospels. In John, the story is not to be separated from the general viewpoint which all the various sections of the Gospel represent. In contrast, the other Gospels repeat tales which have no connecting link in a consistent and chronological impression of Jesus' life. Intuitive judgment can grasp the central aspect of that life from John's account, and can also understand John's own viewpoint and his relationship to his master. Thus, the consistency and chronological sequence of John's Gospel give us grounds

---

10. *Saemmtliche Werke*, part I, vol. 7 (*Hermeneutik*), 172.
11. *Saemmtliche Werke*, part I, vol. 7 (*Hermeneutik*), 174.

for the judgment that generally the author was an eyewitness of the events in his Gospel, and that we have the unified work of a single author before us.

Further considerations about the authenticity of the Gospels will be raised in a later section.[12] Here, it is discussed merely to show how the divinatory method leads to a preference for John among the four evangelists. In John's writing, there is a life-unity to be grasped which is more clearly delineated than in the personalities of the other authors. Christ's work and personality are also more consistently drawn in John than elsewhere.

The work of hermeneutics proceeds in a logical circle. The sense of the individual event is to be found in the setting in which it is placed. Only when the universal whole is comprehended is the single part of that whole understood. But one can approach the whole only by way of the individual. This is obvious in a philological approach: a word is understood only in a sentence, and a sentence only within the context of the whole composition; but to understand the composition, one must read the words and sentences. Schleiermacher extended this hermeneutical circle beyond philology by giving it a psychological setting: a written composition can only be understood in the context of the life history of the author, but that life history can only be understood by observing the entirety of his speech, both oral and written, together with his acts. Understanding is always a constant alternation between consideration of the individual and the whole, so that the circle of relationships in which the individual is set becomes wider and wider.

As an attempt to break the hermeneutical circle, the Roman Catholic Church has put forward the claim of ecclesiastical authority, and Protestant scholasticism the principle of the unity and consistency of the Bible. Schleiermacher believed that such dogmatic claims did not solve the problem, but merely achieved a relative narrowing of the circle. Instead, he saw the problem of interpretation as a never-ending one, understanding the whole in the comprehension of the parts, placing the parts in the setting of the whole. Understanding is found through feeling, by the sympathetic imagination of the interpreter who can intuitively grasp the meaning of both the whole and the parts by the divinatory method. Hermeneutics is an art and brings understanding to completion, much as a work of art is completed.

There are some special problems involved in the interpretation of ancient texts like the Bible. They are written in a foreign language, and their circumstances are beyond the grasp of any ordinary reader. But in principle, the hermeneutical problem is no different from that of the interpretation of other texts: the task is for the interpreter to go back to the original relationship between the speaker and the hearer, between the author and the reader.

12. See ch. 4.

In the original situation, foreign language will not have been a problem, although in every case, the thought-pattern of the creator will be somewhat different from that of the observer. In a relative sense, a work of translation is always necessary. It is necessary to grasp the shape and basis of the differences between author and reader, and this task is the task of psychological interpretation.

Psychological interpretation is the means of putting oneself in the place of the original reader approaching a literary composition. We need to know his point of view and his interest in what is written. We also need to set ourselves in the place of the original author and reconstruct his thought and his approach to writing. Exposition of his thought depends upon this reconstruction, but the basic problem is not that of exposition, but that of understanding. Nothing is more characteristic of human converse than misunderstanding. We regularly misunderstand the speech of those around us and those whose works we read; we also misunderstand them as persons. Schleiermacher says that the task of hermeneutics can be stated in a negative manner:

> Misunderstanding ought to be avoided.... Misunderstanding is self-productive, and at each point understanding must be wished for and sought out.... What is to be avoided is two-fold, the misunderstanding of content, and the misunderstanding of tone.[13]

To avoid misunderstanding and to achieve real understanding of the thought of an author, we must set ourselves in his place. Knowing the circumstances of his life and thought, we must use our sympathetic imagination to grasp the totality of his person, and the particular writing we are considering as a part of that totality. The task is not so much to know the facts of history as to know the person who writes or who has been written about in history.

Like his starting point in religion, the starting point of literary interpretation for Schleiermacher is in personal life. The point is made in a variety of ways and expressed by characteristic words. Hermeneutics is an art depending upon sympathy and imagination for its success. It proceeds by intuition, using methods which are called divinatory and psychological. It is the psychological aspect of the *Hermeneutics* which received the attention of those who continued the discussion of the points it raises. Dilthey was the man who drew most heavily from this aspect of Schleiermacher's thought, and it was this psychological approach which he stressed. Other interpreters

---

13. *Saemmtliche Werke*, part I, vol. 7 (*Hermeneutik*), 29–30.

have approached hermeneutics in the same way. Recently a change of emphasis has been noticeable in the discussion. Under the influence of Hans-Georg Gadamer and Heinz Kimmerle, attention is now being given to the basis of Schleiermacher's hermeneutics in the philosophy of language.[14] Kimmerle's conclusion is that in his earlier work Schleiermacher had based his hermeneutical position on the development of language, and that only in the last decade of his life did he give precedence to the psychological aspect. However, it is easy to overstress the psychological aspect, even in the later period. Schleiermacher's own theory of interpretation requires that one look at an author from as many different points of view as possible, and consider the variety of his writing. As applied to Schleiermacher himself, this would mean that his theory of interpretation should not be drawn from the *Hermeneutics* alone. The grouping together of hermeneutics and textual criticism in his scheme of lectures is significant. Schleiermacher was a dialectical thinker, approaching a subject now from one side, then from another. No one approach can claim to represent the full substance of his thinking. Thus, while it may be true that the real originality of his hermeneutical approach lay in the psychological method, nevertheless it must be remembered that he balanced this with the grammatical method and linked the whole enterprise to historical critique. His approach was never wholly psychological.

INTERPRETING PAUL: AN EXAMPLE FROM *INTRODUCTION TO THE NEW TESTAMENT*

An example of the application of Schleiermacher's hermeneutical principles is provided in his *Introduction to the New Testament*.[15] Written as a course of lectures in 1829 and revised for delivery in 1831 and 1832, it represents his thinking in the vintage period of his theological writing. In the same period, he was revising and editing his major works from previous years. *The Christian Faith*, the *Brief Outline*, and the *Addresses on Religion* all appeared in their final form in 1830 and 1831. It is in this period that Kimmerle has traced the strengthening of the psychological tendency in Schleiermacher's treatment of hermeneutics. In *Introduction*, Schleiermacher sets forth the

---

14. Gadamer, *Wahrheit und Methode*, 174, the section on "Schleiermachers Entwurf einer universalen Hermeneutik." Kimmerle's work is discussed by James Robinson in his article "Hermeneutic since Barth," in Robinson and Cobb, *New Hermeneutic*, 70–71.

15. *Saemmtliche Werke*, part I, vol. 8 (*Neue Testament*).

task of interpretation in a way which is thoroughly consistent with the principles of his *Hermeneutics*:

> Each piece of writing must be set out in such a way that it can be completely understood by those for whom it was originally intended. A writer does not need to take account of anyone else as he writes. Later readers have to put themselves in the place of those whom the author had in mind, and the matter will be consistent and understandable for later readers insofar as they are able to do this. Thus, the task arises for us, as far as it is possible, to put ourselves in the place of the original readers for whom the New Testament authors were writing.[16]

In order to accomplish this purpose, he begins with a historical study of the canon and the text of the New Testament, proceeds to special consideration of its various sections, and concludes with a discussion on sources and literary structure. There is no special psychological emphasis evident in this outline of the subject.

The special introduction of the New Testament books begins with the Pauline letters, because of their chronological priority in the early church.[17] An examination of Schleiermacher's treatment of Paul provides an example of hermeneutics in practice, which complements the theory and allows us to see the balance of Schleiermacher's thought. He begins by setting the collection of Pauline Letters alongside the information contained in Acts and in early Christian histories. He maintains that there is a historical tradition within the church, older than the book of Acts itself, which attributes the founding of a number of congregations to Paul—and this tradition, together with the Acts, provides independent evidence concerning the life and character of the writer of the Epistles.

A comparison of Acts with historical books of the period gives no reason for suggesting that Paul's speeches were spurious compositions, written as exercises in rhetoric like many speeches attributed to classical authors. The speeches and events recorded in Acts can only be properly compared with the contents of the letters. The more the two groups of material agree, the greater is the probability that both are authentic; the more they diverge, the more necessary it is to seek other evidence, and the greater the suspicion that arises against both. Acts records that Paul was a Jew from Tarsus who was educated in Jerusalem under Rabbi Gamaliel. This is in agreement with the remarks which Paul makes in the letters about his upbringing, his strict background, and his zeal as a member of the pharisaic party. He underwent a violent conversion experience, which changed him from

---

16. *Saemmtliche Werke*, part I, vol. 8 (*Neue Testament*), 7.
17. *Saemmtliche Werke*, part I, vol. 8 (*Neue Testament*), 120–94. See sections 33–54.

a persecutor of the church into the leader and great champion of gentile missions, and testimony to this effect is found in both sources. His life as a Christian can be divided into periods, from his conversion until his crossing into Europe, from that point until his imprisonment, and a final period up until his death. This general chronology drawn from Acts is the framework into which the letters can be fitted, and some incidental bits of information about Roman administration link the two accounts to events of the day without giving any positive dates. In some cases, events mentioned in the letters are not referred to in Acts, but this is understandable because Acts does not contain a complete account of Paul's life or work. Many questions can be raised about his journeys, which are not dealt with in either place. Some later traditions are recorded in early ecclesiastical histories, but they merely add information of doubtful authenticity to what we may already know from Acts and the letters. A rough time sequence for the letters may be established on the basis of the three periods of Paul's life as a Christian. Letters carrying instructions and personal greetings to European churches must be dated subsequent to his first arrival in Europe. Those which mention his imprisonment may come from the third period, although some of them could be making reference to an earlier arrest, but those which do not mention prison are probably earlier than his arraignment before Felix. Schleiermacher regarded 1 Thessalonians as the earliest of Paul's letters which we have, written on his first European journey, followed by 1 and 2 Corinthians, and Romans, which was probably the last letter before his imprisonment. Ephesians, Philippians, Colossians, Philemon, and 2 Timothy are letters written from prison, while 1 Timothy, 2 Thessalonians, and Titus are without enough indications for even approximate placing in time. It seems likely that other letters were written by Paul which have not survived. Of those that we have, ten were attested by Marcion, and Schleiermacher gives his estimate of the value of the ancient citations of each of the letters.

Apart from such external witness to the authenticity of Paul's letters, each has an inner character which is of even greater importance. Some are business letters written under the pressure of emergencies in the life of a congregation, like those to Corinth and Galatia. Others are written because of an inclination to give witness to Paul's conception of Christianity, and to commend his ideas to congregations which he founded, like that in Philippi, or ones he had not yet visited, like that in Rome. The inner characteristics are those which show the development of an author's ideas and provide evidence of authenticity by their consistency with what we know of the author from other sources. Just as the events of Paul's life as depicted in Acts roughly correspond to what we know from the Epistles, so the picture of his character which we have from the two sources is a consistent one. The conversion experience on the road to Damascus is only one of a number of ecstatic experiences of which we have an indication, both in the Acts and the letters. Paul's thought regularly proceeds in a dialectical manner, and this displays the characteristics of his psychology. Apparently, Paul's violent persecution of the church was contrary to the advice of his own teacher, Gamaliel, and this conflict of opinion was a preparation for Paul's complete change of direction. In his new role as Christian preacher, he was the foe of any attempt to confine the church to the Jewish race, or to Jewish ritual observance. The manner of Paul's conversion seems to have been an important factor in his becoming the advocate of the universal significance of the Christian faith. In his letters, Paul repeats this theme over and over again, making the contrast of law and gospel a major point in his presentation of the gospel.

Such inner characteristics, in Schleiermacher's view, cannot of themselves establish the authenticity of a composition as the work of a particular author. The historical evidence of external witnesses must precede any judgment on the basis of internal consistency. But historical evidence may be compiled endlessly without arriving at any conclusion. After a thoroughgoing attempt to outline the circumstances surrounding a composition, a judgment based on inner characteristics becomes possible and necessary. When one has knowledge of a man's whole life, one can make a highly probable judgment about whether he did some particular act on the basis of its consistency with his life and character. It is the same with the attribution of a piece of writing to an author: To what extent is it consistent with what we know about him in other respects? Schleiermacher calls the testimony of witnesses the external standard of authenticity, while the internal standard includes the whole matter of the consistency of the composition with what we know of the author's life and thought. In the case of letters, such as those of Paul, the inner standard also includes the consistency of the writing with what we know of the people for whom the letter was composed. Paul turned from being an opponent of Christianity into a preacher of the gospel and missionary to the potential convert—such is the external witness: "This provides a very definite character which must also display itself in his letters. The more this is the case, the stronger is the conviction of their genuineness."[18] The marks of Paul's education among the Pharisees and his desire for mission among the gentiles are present in all his letters. They are strongest in those letters whose claim to genuineness is best, namely, Romans, Galatians, 1 Thessalonians, and 1 and 2 Corinthians. These letters are authenticated by their content and by their agreement with the account

---

18. *Saemmtliche Werke*, part I, vol. 8 (*Neue Testament*), 147.

in Acts: they present the universality of the gospel, and present facts which are consistent with those reported by Luke. In Schleiermacher's view, these five books form the standard against which to measure the claims of any other work attributed to Paul. They complement each other and the Acts by providing facts and conceptions which fill this standard of interpretation, but the discrepancies are minor compared with the general agreement on matters of fact and viewpoint.

Other letters are not so well supported as the five standard ones. Second Thessalonians represents a complete change of view from the thoughts expressed in 1 Thessalonians and 1 Corinthians about the end of the world. The latter two give no indication that the end is very near, yet the former letter makes this the major emphasis for exhortation. Schleiermacher rejects the Pauline authorship of 2 Thessalonians and also of 1 Timothy. Second Timothy and Titus are uncertain, and Schleiermacher cannot find convincing reasons for retention or for rejection. He accepts Philippians, Colossians, and Philemon, but thinks Ephesians might have been written by someone else under Paul's direction. Thus, the Pauline corpus, in his view, definitely contains eight books, with three others as possible additions, two having been definitely rejected. The final standard by which the authenticity of the letters is judged is the personality of Paul. It is at this point that the divinatory method of interpretation becomes most relevant. We need to understand the true individuality of Paul in the totality of his relationships and the entirety of his speech. The content of all his letters must be kept in mind, together with what we know of him from Acts and from such further tradition as we consider genuine. The psychological interpretation which we make of Paul as a man becomes the basis for the historical judgment concerning the authenticity and value of some of the writings attributed to him: "If we concern ourselves with regard to the signs of genuineness of the content of the Pauline Letters, then we come back to his personality with which that content must agree."[19] The basis for our judgment about his personality includes all the records we have of him, telling us of his origin, his education, his relationships to other people at various times in his life, and his own personal development in the midst of these various circumstances. The variety of these records has already been noted, and from them we get a remarkably consistent picture which allows us to set ourselves in his place and reconstruct the development of his thought. A knowledge of the life of the various cities of Greece and Asia Minor helps us to imagine the situation in the congregations to which he wrote and the way in which his letters would be received by the members of the church. All of this is part of our

---

19. *Saemmtliche Werke*, part I, vol. 8 (*Neue Testament*), 176.

understanding of Paul—and the basis on which we can expound his ideas in a modern setting.

This inner conception of Paul is not an outline of his theology. Schleiermacher, as we have seen, did consider that Paul's thinking on the relationship of law and gospel had roots in his psychological makeup, and that the manner of his conversion was another facet of this same aspect of his personality. There are evident links between Paul's character and the categories he used for expounding the gospel. But the discussion of Paul's inner nature does not require the exposition of all his theological ideas, nor is this inner nature the source of the content of his preaching. Paul's preaching was centered upon redemption in Christ and the new life which was available to those who relied upon faith. The understanding and exposition of the preaching depends on our comprehension of the total person of Paul.

Schleiermacher regarded the divinatory method of interpretation as indispensable for understanding, but we can see from the foregoing that it is not the whole of interpretation. His discussion of Paul spends more time dealing with matters of historical fact and grammatical construction than it does upon his personality. But that personality is the key to the free and creative aspect of Paul's life and thought. Without an understanding of that personality, our interpretation is inadequate, because we are left with a mass of disconnected facts and words without any unity in the life of the person concerned. This is the essence of Schleiermacher's psychological interpretation, which approaches every personal act and verbal expression with the question about the real life-unity which lies behind it. There are times in his writings when this psychological tendency becomes so strong that facts and events seem to be unimportant, if not entirely irrelevant. However, such cannot be a balanced view of Schleiermacher's hermeneutical position. Whatever the developments in hermeneutics subsequent to his day, Schleiermacher did not pursue psychological study for its own sake, nor did he dissolve all of his ideas in theology or literature in psychological categories. The divinatory method was the final and most powerful tool for use in the work of interpreting ancient literature. Schleiermacher's edition of Plato, his two volumes of New Testament commentary, and his ten volumes of sermons all attest to the practical use to which he put it. Psychological interpretation had wider implications for Schleiermacher's thought than that of a mere literary tool, but his interpretation of the New Testament rested on more than his psychological viewpoint.

INTERPRETING PAULINE DOCTRINE

The application of Schleiermacher's hermeneutical principles is further exemplified by the treatment afforded to some passages of the Pauline Letters in *Introduction to the New Testament* and in his sermons. As we have seen, Schleiermacher did not think it necessary to outline Paul's doctrine in a thorough manner in order to understand his personality. However, the mark of his personality is to be found in his presentation of doctrine, and the separation of his ideas between his vital teachings and the less important remarks is aided by an understanding of his personality. In *Introduction to the New Testament*, he maintains that there is no more difficult task in interpreting Paul than separating Paul's own teaching from extraneous material which represents the general ideas current in Jewish and Hellenistic thought in his day:

> Among all the New Testament authors there is no one so abundant in ideas as Paul. From no one has arisen so many elements which have been fruitful in the development of Christian doctrine. But also there is no other, in the consideration of whose writings one must guard oneself so carefully against tearing statements out of their particular contexts, and combining them with later presentations whose circumstances are different. There is, therefore, no recommended method for the study of the Pauline writings other than seeking out the general tendency of each individual letter. This will make the composition clear, and enable the main concern of the letter to be separated from what remains. From the main points with which he deals explicitly a total impression may be gained, and we can learn what is his direct concern. What appears to be secondary can be validated only in so far as one finds other places where it is the object of explicit consideration. In this regard the letters to the Romans, Galatians and Colossians remain the most important for dogmatics. In the first and last of these the Apostle is concerned with the general presentation of his method, more extensively in Romans, more concisely in Colossians. In Galatians, however, he sets out from a single point, and that point for him was the central one.[20]

The point from which Galatians sets out is the contrast between law and gospel, and this is the central point in Schleiermacher's consideration of Paul's theology. With the acknowledgment of Christ, the religious value of the law is set aside. Christ was put to death under the law, and thus the

---

20. *Saemmtliche Werke*, part I, vol. 8 (*Neue Testament*), 190–91.

law has lost its power to show forth the will of God. The strength of this theological argument is reinforced by Paul's own personal experience. His education and his own position as a leader among the Pharisees show that in his former life, he was a zealot in the observance of the law. But the law was unable to achieve the blessing which had been promised by God. In his conversion, Paul realized that the law had lost its power, and that those who had formerly sought to obey the law must cease to acknowledge it when they acknowledged Christ. Christ's obedience to the law had abrogated the law, and to continue to honor the law was to dishonor Christ. This is the meaning of Paul's phrase that through the law he had died to the law (Gal 2:9).

In his consideration of Paul's theology in *Introduction to the New Testament*, Schleiermacher regards Galatians as central to Paul's thought, and regards the formulation of its remarkable teaching about the relationship of law and faith as deeply rooted in Paul's own experience. Paul's eagerness in pursuit of the gentile mission is a consequence of this teaching and is similarly grounded in his own life. He had abandoned his former allegiance to the Jewish law, but in Abraham he found a figure whose significance for religion remained secure. Abraham is important as the example of a man of faith, and what was required of him by God is required of those who put their trust in Jesus Christ. The law of Moses was something instituted among the Jewish people in order to isolate them from others around them, and to serve as a defence against the corruption of their conception of God. It still retained a certain validity as a political and social code among those of Jewish descent within Palestine, but it no longer had any religious significance. With the abolition of the law, the restriction of God's promise to those who were descendants of Abraham was lifted. The promise was extended to all who would respond in faith. Therefore, Paul resisted all attempts to make gentile Christians observe Jewish laws: they must be received in the church on the same basis as Jewish Christians without any requirement of Jewish practice. The whole discussion is based on Galatians, although Schleiermacher makes only one direct reference to a verse.[21]

Schleiermacher notes the remarkable way in which Paul is able to extend the idea of law beyond the law of Moses to include all kinds of civil and moral custom. Mosaic law included political, social, and religious legislation, all of which were ascribed to a common theocratic origin. However, political and social elements were a common feature of community law, whether in Jewish or gentile societies. They provided a standard of moral judgment, which could only serve in a preparatory way in order to arouse a consciousness of the need for redemption. The divine revelation in Christ

---

21. *Saemmtliche Werke*, part I, vol. 8 (*Neue Testament*), 81.

put general human law of this kind aside in the same way as it dismissed the Mosaic code.

In his sermons, Schleiermacher also makes the contrast of law and gospel the first point in his consideration of Paul's theology. As in the *Introduction to the New Testament*, his starting point is the consideration of Galatians. In 1830, he preached a series of sermons in commemoration of the presentation of the Augsburg Confession. Two of them are based on the second chapter of Galatians, and both deal with the relationship of law and gospel.[22] Schleiermacher defines justification by faith as the essence of Christianity. For Paul this meant the end of his former life, which was bound to the Jewish law. In the second of these sermons on Galatians 2:19–21, Schleiermacher contends that living on the basis of law and living for the sake of Christ are incompatible with one another, and that this is what is meant by Paul's phrase that through the law he has died to the law so that he may live unto God. The phraseology, he admits, is difficult. Seen in the context of the rest of Galatians and of the letter to the Romans, its meaning may be clearly seen. Christ had died through the action of the law. Those who had been responsible for his death had acted out of zeal for the law, but their zeal was lacking in understanding. By causing the death of Christ, the law had revealed its essential weakness: although its origin was spiritual and its intention was to serve God's good pleasure, its application was a perversion of the will of God. Thus, because of the action of the law, Paul has separated himself entirely from the work of the law. He has renounced his former life and begun a new life in which Christ dwells within him. Schleiermacher's application of these ideas in his sermon is that justification by faith means that we have Christ's life within us as the true principle of our lives. If we truly receive the grace of God, we must reject the law completely, and rely on nothing else in the sight of God except the life of Christ within us.

The first of these sermons had Galatians 2:16–18 as its text-preceding verses, but Schleiermacher refers to Galatians 3:21 for his principal argument concerning the law: "Is the law then opposed to the promises of God? Certainly not! For if a law had been given that could make alive, then righteousness would indeed come through the law" (NRSV). Schleiermacher explains this as meaning that the nature of law is such that it can produce only dead works and not living faith. This is a principle of general application and refers to all kinds of law. The peculiar character of the law of Moses was that it included religious law and civil law in a single code. Thus, what Paul says about the law of Moses must apply equally to the two aspects.

---

22. "On the Augsburg Confession III and IV"; on Galatians 2:16–18, see *Saemmtliche Werke*, part II, vol. 2 (*Vierte-Siebente Sammlung*), 637–52; on Galatians 2:19–21, see 653–65.

Schleiermacher refers generally to the Letter to the Romans, and its placing of Jews and gentiles on the same level with respect to the gospel as corroboration that Paul's remarks apply both to Jewish ordinances and every other kind of code. Thus, civil law and rational law are both included in Paul's general condemnation of reliance upon legislation. The real reason for rejecting law is that obedience to the law can never bring our hearts to the love of God:

> All righteousness is barren where love of God from the heart is lacking. . . . Love knows no law; for it is not within man's capability to decide for himself to love or not, nor can a man be awakened to love by hope or fear, which is the manner in which law encourages or discourages men. Before God's love was poured out, the law ruled legitimately, as the Apostle says, not so that men might be made righteous thereby, but so that by the law there might be aroused in them the consciousness that the present condition was not the right one, and the desire be kindled for a better one. Now, however, the love of God has been poured out in the hearts of believers, since God has proclaimed and commended his love through the sending of his Son. By faith in him another righteousness has been established. In order that we may rejoice in this perfect condition and be encouraged in faith it is necessary that we sharply distinguish the two periods, the time of preparation under the law, and the time of fulfilment beyond the law. Those who are ruled by the Spirit are not under the law.[23]

The contrast between law and gospel was, for Schleiermacher, the key to the understanding of Paul. Its expression was based on Paul's own experience of conversion, and its general influence is to be found in most characteristic doctrines of Paul's theology. It also became a general principle for Schleiermacher's system of thought, and we will find various echoes of the contrast in succeeding chapters. Law and gospel, dead letter and living spirit, outward fact and inward feeling were all concepts by which Schleiermacher extended this contrast into a general principle of theology. With respect to Paul, Schleiermacher used the contrast to explain the discussion of flesh and spirit, the frustration of the natural order of the world, and the new life of a man in Christ. One example is his interpretation of 2 Corinthians 5:17—to speak of the work of Christ as a new creation which may be seen both as the origination of a new humanity, and as the completion of the original work of creation.[24] The new life, despite many characteristics which

---

23. *Saemmtliche Werke*, part II, vol. 2 (*Vierte-Siebente Sammlung*), 644–45.
24. *Christian Faith*, vol. 2, (89:1) 366–67, (106:1) 476–77, (96:3) 396–98;

link it to the old life, is nevertheless lived by a new standard and considered under new concepts. In the new life, as we have seen, the standard of law no longer applies. Christ provides a creative impulse in human life which marks an entirely new beginning. Verse 19 of this chapter provides a phrase which, together with John 1:14, is fundamental to Schleiermacher's conception of Christ: "God was in Christ." For Schleiermacher, this means that the existence of God in Jesus Christ was the central aspect of his personality, the one element in his being to which everything else was related, and which was the organizing principle of everything else. Here is to be found the new creation, and those who are in Christ share in this new creation. The new creation is not under law, but under grace, and entrance to it comes not by works but by faith. It is Christ's work and not our work.

The contrast of law and gospel and the doctrine of the new creation are regarded by Schleiermacher as central in Paul's thought because they are a reflection of Paul's personality and experience. Other doctrines, which have no such personal link, may be accorded less importance. Thus, Schleiermacher regarded the concept of the wrath of God as contrary to the true spirit of Christianity. Any expressions about the wrath of God in Paul's letters are to be ascribed to his description of the time of preparation under the law, and thus applicable only to those who have not come to know Christ. The wrath of God had a basis in Paul's own experience only prior to his conversion, and thus the concept is not part of genuine Christian preaching.[25]

The distinction between Paul's essential teaching and theological concepts derived from non-Christian thought depends on divinatory interpretation. An understanding of Paul as a man is necessary for an understanding of his teaching. Thus, the subjective side of the work of interpretation is a very important part of practical hermeneutics. If we do not understand Paul's personality, we will be unable to make the necessary judgment concerning his theology, and we will fail both in understanding and in communicating his teaching. Our conception of his personality depends upon our knowledge of the relevant facts of his life, together with a thorough grasp of the literary aspects of the expression of his thought. Thus, the divinatory method of interpretation depends on the appreciation of the objective characteristics of a literary work and its author. The subjective basis of interpretation requires a prior judgment of the objective factors. Proper interpretation rests upon both subjective and objective factors, and to give one or the other an exclusive priority will destroy the validity of judgment.

Vierte-Siebente Sammlung, 34, 725; *Saemmtliche Werke*, part II, vol. 3 (*Predigten*), 347.

25. *Saemmtliche Werke*, part II, vol. 2 (*Vierte-Siebente Sammlung*), 725. See "On the Augsburg Confession IX."

4

The Gospels as History

WHAT IS THE SOURCE of Schleiermacher's conception of Christ? His rejection of knowledge as a function of religion would suggest that historical knowledge about Christ is valueless, and that therefore the Gospels as historical records are irrelevant to faith. This seems to be Brunner's point of view when he states that Schleiermacher is concerned only with the "how" of faith and not with the "what," and that Schleiermacher's concept of faith refers only to pious sensations which make no claim to objective truth.[1] However, we have already seen that Schleiermacher gives great importance to the life of Christ and to the Gospels as historical records of that life. In general, Schleiermacher regards the Gospels as objective reports of facts and events and conversations. We have seen how Schleiermacher's subjective judgment about Paul depends upon the objective determination of such facts about Paul's life as are possible to ascertain. A similar procedure is applicable for Schleiermacher in the case of Christ: facts about his life must be determined by the most careful historical and critical investigation, but in themselves, facts are not enough. From the facts we may gain a total impression, which goes beyond the facts to an intuitive response of faith. Facts cannot establish faith, but they may provide the occasion by which faith is aroused. More important than facts is the witness borne to the spiritual reality of Christ in the preaching of the church. This preaching is based upon the

---

1. Brunner, *Die Mystik und das Wort*, 24, 1.

original words and deeds of Christ, which were his own self-proclamation.[2] Thus, the historical reliability of the Gospels is an essential factor in the ongoing proclamation of the church.

The importance of the historical nature of the Gospels is very clear in *The Christian Faith*, although many commentators overlook this because of the more startling propositions which are based on psychology. This chapter will deal with Schleiermacher's conception of the historicity of the Gospels in *The Christian Faith* and also in some of his critical writings about the New Testament. His first work of New Testament criticism, published in 1807, deals with 1 Timothy.[3] Others include the *Essay on Luke* of 1817, *Introduction to the New Testament*, and his article "On Colossians 1:15–20," published in 1832. These works are generally ignored in discussions of Schleiermacher's theology, but they should not be regarded as isolated or uncharacteristic works. Terrence Tice, in his *Schleiermacher Bibliography*, mentions "many series of exegesis lectures, among the unpublished manuscripts in the Literatur-Archiv in Berlin."[4] Until these are consulted, any conclusions about his exegesis must remain tentative. However, the importance of the historical reliability of the Gospels is clearly shown in the works which are available. In this chapter, consideration will be given to his *Essay on Luke*, *Introduction to the New Testament*, and to his sermons on the raising of Lazarus from the *Homilies on John*.

THE CHRISTIAN FAITH

In *The Christian Faith*, at the conclusion of the discussion on "The Person of Christ," Schleiermacher has a brief section on New Testament Christology, which is the epitome of his approach to the whole of the New Testament.[5] In it, he affirms the historicity and trustworthiness of the New Testament as a whole, while outlining the limits imposed on the credit to be given to individual passages because of critical exegetical methods. Schleiermacher asserts that the faith of the church of his day concerning the person of Christ is that of the faith held originally in the early church, and that its basis is Christ's sayings about himself. The authentication of faith here has three distinct parts: one is that Christ's statements are fundamental to faith and were accurately reported by his hearers; secondly, that the doctrine

---

2. *Christian Faith*, vol. 1 (19:1), 88–89.

3. *Saemmtliche Werke*, part I, vol. 2, *Ueber den sogenannten ersten Brief des Paulos an den Timotheos*, 223–320.

4. Tice, *Schleiermacher Bibliography*, 9.

5. *Christian Faith*, vol. 2 (99), 421–24.

of the ancient church reflects the proper interpretation of the records; and finally, that Schleiermacher's own presentation of the teaching of the person of Christ as representative of Christian thought from his own day is in essence a faithful restatement of what Christ and the early Christians had already said.

The essential point in the development of his argument is his basic point about matters of interpretation: "Faith . . . was not based on details, but develops out of a total impression."[6] It is not individual sayings of Christ which are important, or particular verses, or any special group of New Testament books. Christ was believed by his followers because of the impression he made in the totality of his relationships with them. It is not the particular presentation made by a New Testament writer, or a phrase in one of the creeds, or even the creeds themselves which can witness to the beliefs of the early Christians; it is the total impact of their doctrine, preaching, and way of life, which is the attestation of the faith of the early church. It is not the repetition of ancient phrases or the inclusion of all the decisions of ancient councils, or even the strict observation of the letter of the New Testament, which can establish a modern statement of faith as orthodox; it is the total impression gained from the contemporary faith viewed from every side which allows one to judge if its content is the same as that of the original faith.

It is in the light of this principle of interpretation that Schleiermacher deals with the problems of exegesis. In the first place, it is clear that later statements do not merely repeat what earlier statements have said. This is accounted for by the necessary development of understanding and terminology, so that subsequent formulations take account of sophistications in language and distinctions within teaching which were previously unnecessary. Such development is legitimate, provided it is not demonstrably at variance with the original doctrines. Within this development, there remain differing accounts of how individual books of the New Testament came into being, who their authors were, and how they are to be used for preaching and teaching. Because of such disputes, it is not possible to rely upon any one text for the support of a particular doctrine, but a basis must be found within the whole of the New Testament. Schleiermacher regards this wider basis as a proper safeguard against the danger of someone reading one's own ideas into the New Testament: he believes that the essential doctrines would be discernible by "anyone who in the interpretation of particular passages is not content merely with a sense in harmony with his own theory, but keeps

---

6. *Christian Faith*, vol. 2 (99), 423.

an open mind for a true impression of the whole."⁷ It is on this basis that Schleiermacher regards himself as a loyal interpreter of the gospel, faithfully expounding the main sense of the New Testament and not presenting merely his own private theory. Modern discussion of Schleiermacher has centered around this particular point. Very clearly, Schleiermacher believes his own reading of the New Testament to be a true impression of the whole of the gospel message, arrived at without undue reliance upon his own theories. Yet it will be seen that Schleiermacher's judgment of the value of passages in the Gospels—the meanings given to words in his outline of doctrine, his concept of the person of Christ, and his use of the Old Testament—all depend upon his conception of religion. From a twenty-first-century point of view, his doctrine and preaching display his metaphysical scepticism, his literary romanticism, and his German nationalism. The hermeneutical circle is plainly displayed in all he wrote, and it is evident that he was aware of the problem which has become a central one in our day. It is this awareness, and the efforts he makes to solve the hermeneutical problem, which make Schleiermacher's writings important for modern theology. But his solution is clearly inadequate: to say that one must read the New Testament so as to get a true impression of the whole, free from mere agreement with one's own personal ideas, is to beg the very question it is meant to solve.

Section 131 of *The Christian Faith* sets forth Schleiermacher's general acknowledgment of the New Testament: "As regards their origin the New Testament Scriptures are authentic, and as a norm for Christian Doctrine they are sufficient."⁸ By authenticity, as we have already seen, Schleiermacher means that the New Testament records really do give a record of the words and deeds of Jesus (written by people who had reliable sources of information)—and also a contemporary record of the life of the early church. By sufficiency, Schleiermacher means that there is nothing else we need to know about Christ's life and teaching, or the period after Pentecost, which is not contained in the New Testament as we know it. The important message of the gospel is its inner teaching, which reveals its general intention; for Schleiermacher, no further writings by the original disciples or anyone else can add to or alter this inner value. The Bible is deliberately vague about many details of Jesus' life because these details can add nothing to the inner meaning of the gospel teachings:

> It is a divine provision, certainly of the highest significance, but not sufficiently recognized, that neither a trustworthy tradition regarding the external aspect of Christ's person, nor an authentic

---

7. *Christian Faith*, vol. 2 (99), 422.
8. *Christian Faith*, vol. 2 (131), 64.

picture of it, has come down to us. For the same reason, we may be sure, we lack an exact description of His manner of life and a connected narrative of the events of His career.[9]

Further consideration will be given in a later section to the sufficiency of the gospel record for doctrine; here, attention will be directed to the question of authenticity.

The New Testament, for Schleiermacher, contains an accurate record of the facts of Christ's life and speech, and represents the most correct view of those facts. Its source is the circle of people who had followed Christ during his life in Palestine, and who by close association with and confidence in him accepted the right view of his life and developed his teaching in the proper manner. The writing of the Gospels depended on the memory of the apostles and on the selection by their followers of those memories which were most conducive to the general aim of the apostolic preaching. Some of the narratives are records of incidents which the original author witnessed himself; others are materials put together by someone with no personal experience of the events, yet with sufficient information and a common tendency with the apostles, so that he could produce a record as valuable as that of an eyewitness. Schleiermacher believed that the Gospels as we know them were compilations of previously isolated narratives and that both the authors of the narratives and the narratives' compilers were men in a position to do their work accurately and correctly. This does not mean that the individual books were actually written by the persons whose names they bear. Even in the earliest times, a name other than that of the author's might have been attached to one of our New Testament books, because such an ascription did not offend the moral sense either of the author or of those for whom the book was written. In later times, a book might be wrongly attributed to a certain author because of a mistake on the part of the church. As long as the incorrect attribution was not the result of a deliberate attempt to mislead, Schleiermacher cannot see any objection to the inclusion of the book in the Bible under its familiar title.

Schleiermacher denies it is possible to draw up a list of authors whose works would automatically deserve a place in the canon, nor that it is possible by such means to exclude books by certain classes of people. The authenticity of the New Testament writings means that we trust the universal Christian experience as the testimony of the Holy Spirit that the canon we have received from church tradition has not by deceit or ignorance had introduced into it such constituent parts as belong to either an apocryphal or an heretically suspect zone of Christianity, to which such preeminent

---

9. *Christian Faith*, vol. 2 (98), 417.

dignity could not be ascribed without danger.[10] This is to say that the authenticity of the New Testament is a part of our faith in the work of the Holy Spirit within the church, and that the actual books which compose it may have differing value, both in content and arrangement, and differing justification for their inclusion within the canon.

But the work of the Spirit in this case is the work of proper historical composition. It is not the mere reproduction of memories or the narration of individual facts, but the effort to show Christ as he lived. Christ's teachings consist of conversation and speeches elicited by special circumstances, and these circumstances must be understood in order to gain a complete understanding of the teaching. Therefore, the historical sections of the New Testament are no less important than the material which is more strictly doctrinal. A pure and complete apprehension of many aspects of Christ's life was essential for the early church. The apostles' thinking was shaped by it, and their teaching, as a development of Christ's own preaching, was conditioned by their understanding of the circumstances in which he had spoken. The New Testament which we have is a proper record of Christ's teaching, and provides us with sufficient information concerning his actions, and the people and events of his life, to enable us to gain a total impression of him—and to see the apostolic preaching as the legitimate consequence of what he was and did.

In *The Christian Faith*, Schleiermacher is not directly concerned with the exposition and exegesis of particular passages in the New Testament. This is because of his view of the work as a scientific rather than a scriptural dogmatic. Nevertheless, it is of interest to notice the examples of exegesis which are found within it. At a number of points, the dogmatic value of a creedal statement depends on the judgment rendered about one or two individual passages, and even a scientific dogmatic has to engage in a narrow and specific exegetical task. One instance of this is the discussion of the virgin birth of Jesus, found in section 97 of *The Christian Faith*.[11] Schleiermacher states that this discussion must have two aspects, one dealing with the New Testament material on the subject, the other concerning itself with the dogmatic value of the statement of Christ's conception in a supernatural manner. There are two stories in the Gospels referring to the conception of Christ without any male activity: Matthew 1:18–25 and Luke 1:31–34. No further reference is made to them anywhere else in the New Testament, and Matthew, Luke, and John all contain passages which refer to Jesus as Joseph's son, without a hint of any knowledge of the virgin birth.

---

10. *Christian Faith*, vol. 2 (131:1), 605.
11. *Christian Faith*, vol. 2 (97:2), 403–7.

Thus, the textual support for the doctrine is weak, and it is clear that Christ's original followers set no great value upon it in their preaching, teaching, or writing. In New Testament times, it must have been possible to have had a proper idea of Christ as Redeemer without a belief in his conception in a supernatural manner. If the early tradition about the virgin birth is uncertain, its dogmatic position is even weaker. Neither the Apostles' Creed nor the Nicene deal with it in a way that would give it dogmatic importance. Doctrinally, the important concept is that of the sinless Redeemer in whom the divine and the human are united in a new creation. This has nothing to do with the presence or absence of sexual intercourse. There remains a general idea of supernatural conception, but the virgin birth as such is superfluous from a dogmatic point of view. Its affirmation or denial must be based entirely upon the gospel narratives which have been cited, and it is possible to view these as true, literally and historically—or not—without any effect on the idea of Christ as Redeemer. From this and other passages in his writings, it is clear that Schleiermacher rejects the historical character of the virgin birth.

Another example of exegesis in *The Christian Faith* is the section on New Testament Christology which has already been mentioned.[12] The basic concepts which Schleiermacher uses in interpreting the person of Christ are "essential sinlessness" and "the being of God in him." For the first of these concepts, he refers to John 8:46: "Which of you convicts me of sin?" For the second, he refers to John 10:30–38:

> The Father and I are one. . . . If I am not doing the works of my Father, then do not believe me. But if I do them, even though you do not believe me, believe the works, so that you may know and understand that the Father is in me and I am in the Father. (NRSV)

Neither of these passages by itself can prove the doctrine which he is seeking to establish. The basic concepts are a proper expression of the total impression of the New Testament, and Schleiermacher cites a further series of references, not as proof in themselves, but rather as corroboration of a doctrine already established. In this process, the heaviest reliance is placed upon John's Gospel, which is cited in this section more than all other books of the New Testament put together. The Johannine picture is amply supported by other writers:

> But that the faith even of the first generation of His disciples had the same content as we have set forth here, is proved, not only

---

12. *Christian Faith*, vol. 2 (99), 421–24.

THE GOSPELS AS HISTORY   57

by the most various testimonies which ascribe to Christ's perfect purity and fullness of power, but also by the way in which Paul describes Him, in contrast to Adam, as the originator of a new human worth, and by the Johannine presentation of the λόγος [logos], as well as by the theory set forth in the Epistle to the Hebrews.[13]

Doctrinally, these concepts are of the highest significance, and in Schleiermacher's view they are the central points in the whole discussion of Christology. Christ's sinlessness is an expression of his perfection as a man, and the same point is repeatedly established in a number of ways: the exclusive dignity of Christ is his identity as a person; his life is absolute perfection, absolute purity, and essential sinlessness; his birth is the completion of the creation of human nature. The being of God in Christ is also spoken of in various ways:[14] Christ had an absolutely powerful God-consciousness, and in him there was fullness of power; there is no limit to Christ's influence over the human race; the existence of God in Christ was the center of his personality and the source of all his activity. This concept of the person of Christ is developed from Schleiermacher's general analysis of the religious self-consciousness, together with his understanding of the place of Christ in the faith of Christians, and it is then supported by an interpretation of the general sense of Scripture. It is thus an excellent illustration of Schleiermacher's method: interpretation may start from any one of a number of points of view—systematic, speculative, confessional, or scriptural—but if the interpretation is correct, all of these will ultimately agree in a general impression which proceeds from the same spirit which animated the faith of the earliest Christians.

In most instances in *The Christian Faith*, Schleiermacher does not begin this process of interpretation from biblical citations. He proceeds instead from a few basic propositions which are developed in a way broadly consistent with the general sense of Scripture. Thus, most doctrines are stated in language quite different from Scripture and in a way which prevents them from being attached to any particular passage. It is much easier to find instances where his interpretation contradicts traditional exegesis than ones which support it, because his support is given in general terms while his rejection must be plain in order to avoid pious misinterpretation. For a closer view of his attitude toward New Testament passages, it is necessary to turn to his critical and homiletical works.

13. *Christian Faith*, vol. 2 (99), 423.
14. *Christian Faith*, vol. 2 (96:3), 396–98, (105:3) 468–72, (105) 473–75.

ESSAY ON LUKE

Schleiermacher's *Essay on Luke* was written as the refutation of a thesis that an original gospel, now lost, was the common source of the Synoptic Gospels. Schleiermacher intended to publish a critical examination of Luke's writings, including both the gospel and the book of Acts, but the second part was never written. In place of the theory of a lost gospel, Schleiermacher puts forward the theory that a number of collections of records of Jesus existed in the early church, and that our present gospels of Matthew, Mark, and Luke were dependent upon these. The purpose of written records was to give assistance to preachers of the gospel. In the earliest times, such records were not needed, because the preachers were the apostles, or people who had stood in close relationship with Jesus or were otherwise well acquainted with the circumstances of his ministry. The first written records are attributable to those who had come to believe in Jesus without having known him themselves. These wished to have fuller knowledge of his life so that, as far as possible, they could have the same background for their preaching as their older companions. The first stage in this process would have been the collecting of records of various aspects of Christ's life by various people: speeches, miracle stories, events preceding the crucifixion, references to the resurrection, etc. The actual writing of the Gospels is a later stage and consists of the collecting and editing of these earlier collections. Schleiermacher judges that Matthew and Luke arose in this way, and that their authors had used collections which in some cases were the same, but different in others. The names of the authors are unknown, as no credence is given to the names attached to the books. Generally, Schleiermacher regards Luke as having more reliable sources than did Matthew; he regards Mark as dependent upon Matthew, and thus the least important of the three. Schleiermacher's discussion of the first two chapters of Luke illustrates his conception of the extent and reliability of the preceding collections. The whole of the first chapter, with the exception of the first four verses, he regards as a connected tale which Luke copied into his Gospel without alteration.[15] The final verse of the chapter provides a conclusion to all that has preceded, as if it served to complete a story that was told about Mary and Elizabeth. The whole is a beautiful little work of art:

> So little can I see here a story of literal history . . . so little also would I want to declare the whole to be fabrication. But it seems that the poet has taken the liberty to which he was entitled, and

---

15. *Saemmtliche Werke*, part I, vol. 2 (*Ueber die Schriften des Lukas*), 14–36.

gathered together remote materials, setting forth the slender tradition in bold colour.[16]

Thus, the first chapter of Luke is poetical and not historical in character; its details are not to be relied on. The second chapter is very different. Here, a group of materials has been put together by the editor of the gospel, and while their value varies, some of them are of the highest historical value. The story of Jesus' birth is the most important and also the most reliable. Any poetic tendencies within the story are severely restrained, although from the nature of the story there was opportunity for poetical amplification. The fact that Christ is reported as bedded in a stall is the kind of detail which could never have been invented. The words of the angel are, of course, not literal reports from the time of their appearance, but they are to be accepted as reliable reports of an astonishing experience which happened to the shepherds outside Bethlehem. It is the shepherds themselves who must have been the original source of the whole story:

> We must trace back at least the essence of the story to genuine historical tradition .... It is convincingly probable that the story as we have it here must be traced back to the shepherds as its original source. To the shepherds' story has been added the story of the journey to Bethlehem—to account for the presence of Mary and Joseph in Nazareth.[17]

The circumcision story in verse 21 is an arbitrary addition, but Schleiermacher judges the story of the purification to be historical.[18] Like the birth story, its poetic possibilities are not developed and some of its detail is too remarkable for invention. He attributes the source of this story to someone who heard of the incident from Anna and who remembered it in later years when Jesus was preaching. The story of the Passover visit to Jerusalem when Jesus was twelve may also be historical.[19] Schleiermacher thinks that the compiler of the gospel heard this story directly or indirectly from Mary, and wrote it in his own words at the conclusion of other stories of Jesus' childhood. Throughout, Schleiermacher draws a contrast between the infancy narratives found in Luke and Matthew, and attests the former as historical—as against the latter, which he regards as based on less valuable tradition.[20]

---

16. *Saemmtliche Werke*, part I, vol. 2 (*Ueber die Schriften des Lukas*), 19.

17. *Saemmtliche Werke*, part I, vol. 2 (*Ueber die Schriften des Lukas*), 23–24.

18. *Saemmtliche Werke*, part I, vol. 2 (*Ueber die Schriften des Lukas*), 22, 28.

19. *Saemmtliche Werke*, part I, vol. 2 (*Ueber die Schriften des Lukas*), 31.

20. *Saemmtliche Werke*, part I, vol. 2 (*Ueber die Schriften des Lukas*), 36, 47, 215.

The rest of the gospel is handled in a manner similar to this account of the first two chapters. Luke has a number of records in front of him and generally he reproduces material from these collections without alteration. But Luke's great skill is that of selection, for the material which he includes has an authentic tone which is evident in most cases. For the central portion of the gospel, Luke generally uses a collection containing speeches, and another containing remarkable activities of Jesus. The temptation story is not an account of an event, but a parable told by Jesus. The transfiguration, on the other hand, is an account from one of the three who went up the mountain with Jesus.

The section of the gospel dealing with the Last Supper and the arrest, trial, and crucifixion of Jesus (Luke 22:1–23, 49) is the reproduction of a connected account which Luke had before him.[21] It consists of two main sections—one dealing with the supper, and the other with the arrest and its aftermath—to which have been added a number of smaller incidents of less value and importance. The account of the meal is not really a story of Jesus' last night before his death, but only the account of the institution of the Lord's Supper. But in that context it is a genuine and original account of what happened. The second section is likewise historically valuable. The original writer of the passages about the arrest, trial, and crucifixion was an eyewitness to at least some of the events. He may well have been present among a crowd in the garden of Gethsemane, and his account of the trial is supplemented by information which he received from sources inside Pilate's palace.

The subsequent material in the gospel is of lesser value. The story of Christ's burial was another connected account which the editor found before him and simply tacked onto the account of the death.[22] The important story of the resurrection in Luke is the account of the men who met Jesus on the road to Emmaus. The story of the women at the tomb is simply a later expansion of the tale told by the Emmaus disciples (Luke 24:22–23):

> Moreover, some women of our group astounded us. They were at the tomb early this morning, and when they did not find his body there, they came back and told us that they had indeed seen a vision of angels who said that he was alive. (NRSV)

This account probably ended at 24:43, and the ending of the gospel is to be regarded as an addition.

---

21. *Saemmtliche Werke*, part I, vol. 2 (*Ueber die Schriften des Lukas*), 200–16.
22. *Saemmtliche Werke*, part I, vol. 2 (*Ueber die Schriften des Lukas*), 217.

Among the Synoptic Gospels, therefore, Schleiermacher regarded Luke as the most reliable and most important, and the stories in Luke are given a very high importance as historical sources. But the author was not himself an apostle—nor a participant in or witness of the events which he described. On a number of matters he was mistaken and his reports require correction from other sources, but such correction is needed less by Luke than by Matthew and Mark. The sources of the correction are the writings of Paul and John. Generally, however, Schleiermacher thinks that Luke's accounts can be used as a supplement to Paul and John, and that these three are our sources of information about Christ and the early church.

INTRODUCTION TO THE NEW TESTAMENT: JOHN'S GOSPEL

As we have seen in the discussion of the *Hermeneutics*, Schleiermacher preferred John's Gospel to the Synoptics. The same preference is evident in *Introduction to the New Testament*. John's Gospel is regarded as the most reliable record of the life of Christ:

> We cannot assume that the first three gospels contain a complete coherent history. Rather must we consider them as having been put together out of individual tales which in large part stem from people who did not belong to the closest circle of Jesus' disciples. On the other hand the gospel of John is the result of apostolic authorship.[23]

Schleiermacher accepts the apostle John himself as the author, and does not think that anyone else edited or altered it. After being written, it was retained by the author and circulated only after his death as a very old man. Originally, the gospel ended with chapter 20, and the final chapter was added as an appendix, either by John himself or by a close associate who wrote under John's direction. Throughout the gospel, we have signs which indicate that the author was an eyewitness and participant in the events described.

One such event which marks the closeness of the author of John to the events is the story of the woman at the well near Samaria.[24] The incident was overlooked by other accounts of Jesus' life because its significance rests on a private conversation between Jesus and the woman. The disciples had gone into the city for food, and on their return did not venture to ask Jesus what had occurred when he was talking to her. John, however, as the intimate

---

23. *Saemmtliche Werke*, part I, vol. 8 (*Neue Testament*), 332. See also 278, 283.
24. *Saemmtliche Werke*, part I, vol. 8 (*Neue Testament*), 282.

friend of the master, was told about it and reported it. Other instances where John shows evidence of knowing about Jesus' private friendships are the story of the marriage in Cana and the stories about the household of Martha, Mary, and Lazarus in Bethany. John was an eyewitness of the raising of Lazarus from the grave.[25]

Schleiermacher accepted John's outline of the chronology of Christ's ministry in preference to that of the Synoptic Gospels. The Synoptic account tells of only one visit of Christ to Jerusalem with his followers. The visit therefore has to provide the setting for all of the incidents which they recount in the city and in the surrounding countryside. Christ's friendship with Lazarus's family in Bethany is one circumstance which makes the idea of a single visit unsatisfactory. The cleansing of the temple was not a symbolic act at the end of Christ's life, but was probably something which happened whenever he visited the city: the moneychangers would have been continually encroaching on the reserved areas of the temple and were probably chased out repeatedly by others besides Christ. John is correct in recounting the story early in his account of Christ's ministry. Because of the necessity of setting all of the stories about Jerusalem in the days prior to the crucifixion, some of them have been omitted from the Synoptic accounts, while John is able to record them as part of an earlier visit to the city. Christ's teaching is correctly reported by John, but it has been carefully selected and arranged to present two special aspects: the whole impression of Christ is given as the ground of faith, and his relationship with the religious authorities of his day is developed as a preparation for the final conflict.[26] Thus, Christ's speeches in John have all to do with his presentation as the Messiah and deal with the dignity of his person, his relationship to the Father, and his rejection by the established leaders of the people. Parabolic teaching and proverbial sayings, so common in the other gospels, have been largely omitted, unless they can be closely related to the messianic theme. A great deal of material available to John has been omitted from his gospel because he did not find it relevant to the development of his two main themes. Thus, the book is not a simple recounting of events, but a careful composition arranged with a view to displaying the grace and truth of God in Christ. The prologue to the gospel is an integral part of the whole, in which John gives the briefest and most natural presentation of the revelation which God has made through his word in the human life of Christ. Schleiermacher denies

---

25. *Saemmtliche Werke*, part I, vol. 8 (*Neue Testament*), 282. For Schleiermacher's account of the raising of Lazarus, see the following section. See also ch. 8, "The Reversal of Method." *Neue Testament*, 280.

26. *Saemmtliche Werke*, part I, vol. 8 (*Neue Testament*), 318–19.

the suggestion that its sources should be sought in some outside intellectual circles:

> One can see clearly how this presentation of Christ can have arisen purely on the basis of particular expressions of his, without any need of taking refuge in any idea of a foreign philosophy or Jewish esoteric doctrine. Thus, it is clear that this introduction is based on Christ's speeches, and not the other way around, that Christ's speeches in John are the product of the author, based on his introduction.[27]

In accordance with Schleiermacher's hermeneutical principles, it is the total impression of John's Gospel, rather than any of the particular characteristics or incidents, which attest its authenticity:

> When we consider John's Gospel by itself, without comparing it to the others, the total impression which it makes as a whole is that except for a few additions it is an account by a direct participant, and not something put together out of previously available particulars.[28]

Thus, the value of John's Gospel as a reliable historical source is of the highest character. By comparison, the Synoptic accounts are less valuable, but Luke in particular is a very worthy source and contains much material which can supplement the Johannine story. Luke, like the other Synoptic writers, did not have a reliable account of the chronology of Christ's ministry, but for incidents from his life and selections from his teaching, his sources were very good. Matthew generally requires to be corrected on the basis of Johannine and Lukan material, and is not such a valuable source. Mark was dependent on Matthew, so his material has no independent importance.

These accounts demonstrate the extent to which Schleiermacher regarded the gospel records as authentic, and the importance given to their reliability. There is no suggestion in any of the critical material that the historical documents of Christianity may be dismissed as irrelevant to faith, but they do have to stand the test of critical scrutiny. Not all of the New Testament books can survive the examinations: 1 Timothy is not Pauline, and the Apocalypse is not Johannine. The Apocalypse is not worthy to be used as the basis of Christian teaching, and it is retained in the canon because the canon is fixed and cannot now be altered.[29] Those works which do stand scrutiny are generally accurate records of the life of Christ and of the early church, and they must form the basis of the Christian self-consciousness.

---

27. *Saemmtliche Werke*, part I, vol. 8 (*Neue Testament*), 335.
28. *Saemmtliche Werke*, part I, vol. 8 (*Neue Testament*), 318.
29. *Saemmtliche Werke*, part I, vol. 8 (*Neue Testament*), 470.

Thus, in his critical writings, Schleiermacher reinforces his conclusions in *The Christian Faith* about the authenticity of the New Testament records. Two particular examples of his affirmation of the accounts in the Gospels are the raising of Lazarus and the resurrection of Christ. As is characteristic for Schleiermacher, both are based on John.

THE RAISING OF LAZARUS

In Schleiermacher's opinion, John's story of the raising of Lazarus is the report of an eyewitness. The absence of the story from the Synoptics is a remarkable fact which Schleiermacher uses as evidence that their authors were not part of Jesus' immediate circle.[30]

The three evangelists were ignorant of our Lord's close relationship with this family. Schleiermacher is doubtful if the story of the woman who anointed Jesus in the Synoptics (Mark 14:3–9; Matthew 26:6–13; Luke 7:36–50) refers to the same incident as the story of Mary in John 12. In the former, there is no suggestion that the woman is a close friend and follower of Jesus, nor does the story of Martha and Mary in Luke 10 give any indication of near acquaintance. The entire Synoptic chronology, which is based on the assumption that all of Jesus' ministry took place in Galilee until the journey which ended in his death, prevents the three evangelists from acknowledging that Jesus had close friends in Bethany whose home he frequented. Only John knew this, and unless his gospel is to be regarded as an artificial construction, it must be regarded as the only sustained eyewitness account among the Gospels.

Schleiermacher deals, in 1825, with the eleventh chapter of John in four sermons, part of his series of *Homilies on the Gospel of John*.[31] He remarks that the relationship of Jesus to Lazarus's household was so close that they kept in contact, and the sisters knew where to send for him when Lazarus became ill. The character of the story is typical of John. There is plenty of detail which could only be that of an eyewitness, but John's interest is not centered in the events themselves. Wherever possible, John uses events of the temporal order to point to what is eternal—and stories are included in order to present the Christ in whom we must have faith—and to show how the events of Christ's life generate opposition among the religious leaders, resulting in his arrest and crucifixion. Schleiermacher does not believe that the illness of Lazarus was an event of which Jesus had any foreknowledge, nor does he think Jesus deliberately allowed Lazarus to die in order to work

---

30. *Saemmtliche Werke*, part I, vol. 8 (*Neue Testament*), 282–84.
31. *Saemmtliche Werke*, part I, vol. 8 (*Neue Testament*), 238–91.

a demonstrative miracle. Jesus learns of the illness as any other person would: a messenger comes with the news and asks for Jesus to assist. The Lord's delay in going to Bethany is caused by the demands of his preaching mission beyond the Jordan. This was territory in which John the Baptist had worked effectively, and many of his followers had become believers in Christ. Jesus knows that he will not be able to visit the region again, and so he is compelled to stay until his work is complete. He would not have delayed deliberately, because his love for Lazarus and his family would have prevented him from causing unnecessary suffering to them. Furthermore, the character of his life means that he could use his divine power to help human suffering only in accordance with his divine calling. There is no place in this calling for deliberate self-display. When he does set out for Bethany, he does so with confidence that God will hear his prayer and that no harm will come to Lazarus in the end.

Schleiermacher acknowledges the difficulty which verse 4 makes for this interpretation: it reports what Jesus says when he hears of Lazarus's illness (John 11:4): "But when Jesus heard it, he said, 'This illness does not lead to death; rather it is for God's glory, so that the Son of God may be glorified through it.'" Schleiermacher regards the verse as difficult for any interpretation: if Christ is said to have had foreknowledge of the events, then this implies that he is mistaken. If spiritual death is meant, then Jesus is pictured as deliberately and unnecessarily causing suffering and grief among those whom he is said to love. Schleiermacher suggests that Jesus did not think that Lazarus would die—and in any case, Jesus is prevented from leaving sooner.

Subsequently Jesus learns that Lazarus has died. Schleiermacher suggests that he might have received a second message, or else that he simply became convinced of it in his own mind through his divine consciousness. He knows, then, that he will have to raise Lazarus and that this will be a means of strengthening the faith of his followers:

> The Lord was certainly right in thinking that such a physical image of the power of the resurrection, such a definite and unique occurrence as would appear before their eyes, at all events would have a strong tendency to strengthen the trust of those human hearts which by nature were so weak in faith.[32]

It is not in order to create faith that Christ performs the miracle—those for whom he acts were already believers—but he does seek to strengthen and deepen that faith. Its later effect of causing some of the visitors to the home

---

32. *Saemmtliche Werke*, part II, vol. 9 (*Johannes*), 254

to become believers is merely incidental. The occasion is used to strengthen Martha's faith. John 11:25 says, "Jesus said to her, 'I am the resurrection and the life. Those who believe in me, even though they die, will live'" (NRSV). This has a double significance: on the one hand, there is the assurance in him of resurrection at the last day; on the other hand, there is the everlasting life which is already given to those who believe, in which they are already raised from death to spiritual life. The life which is given to believers is communion with God, in which their will is united to his will, their nature assimilated to his glory. Belief in the Son of God is the same thing as seeing in Christ the glory of God, and directing all human life, whether crude or cultivated, toward the abiding source of all nature.

Schleiermacher's psychological tendency is displayed in his interpretation of the emotion which Jesus shows just before going to the tomb. The psychological viewpoint is not regarded as constitutive, but rather as interpretive of what took place:

> We must remember that the Redeemer had personal reasons connected with his immediate obligations, so that, after receiving the news about Lazarus's illness, he was not able to leave the place where he was any earlier, with the effect that he managed to arrive only after Lazarus had died and had been buried for four days. In a similar way he was unable to know what effect these circumstances would have upon himself. The thing which he intended to do oppressed his spirit and did not leave him unmoved. The action would be a new demonstration of his wonderful power, although he had come with the purpose of exercising it. He lived in a relationship of quiet trust with this power, so the prospect of exercising it lay quietly on his heart. But there were people present for whom he had not wished, and notoriety would arise for which he had not sought. The occasion would give his enemies a new complaint, for he knew well that the people who were present would bring the first news of the extraordinary happening to the High Priests, who were hostile to him, and to the Jewish council. His mind knew about his own death, and the connection between this affair of waking from the dead and the warnings of his own death. These things must have troubled him in a very particular way. Certainly it was the expression of such contradictory emotions which John presents for us in a few words, in the unsurpassable manner in which he describes such things through clear and exact language. What at least he tells us is of the inner struggle between

these contradictory human emotions in the disposition of the Redeemer.[33]

This paragraph is an outstanding example of the divinatory mode of interpretation: it is an attempt to project the mind of Christ as he approached a turning-point in his ministry. It rests on only a few words in the text of verses 33 and 38:

> Jesus . . . was greatly disturbed in spirit and deeply moved. . . .
> Then Jesus, again greatly disturbed, came to the tomb. (NRSV)

The basis for this projection is a concept of Christ's mind as human in its emotional makeup and limited to human knowledge of facts, but entirely confident in dependence upon God as the source of power and of will. In this situation, at least, Schleiermacher does not use a psychological projection to displace things reported as facts. He accepts as fact that Lazarus was raised from the dead, and regards John as an accurate witness of what happened at the tomb.

In accordance with John's own practice, attention is diverted immediately from the events to their significance. Thus, there is no description of what Lazarus said to Jesus, or of the reaction of the family or the crowd. Instead, we are told how the event was significant for belief or disbelief among those who saw and heard. Schleiermacher's account of what happened at the open grave is interesting as an example of what he meant by the absolute God-consciousness of Jesus:

> That which first attracts our attention in this text, the miracle of the re-awakening of Lazarus, is something about which no one knows what to say, because it is hidden from our eyes. What we do know about it are the words of the Lord himself to which we need also to pay close attention. He lifted up his eyes as the stone was removed from the grave and said, "Father, I thank you that you have heard me; yet I know that you always hear me."
>
> Thus, in the first instance, he was certain not that somehow Lazarus would come back to life, but that already he had come back to life, because he said, "I thank you that you have heard me." Let us note that he did not ascribe this miracle to himself as his own direct action upon Lazarus, and in this connection he had done nothing visible or audible. On the contrary he ascribed the miracle to his Father, although it was done at his

---

33. *Saemmtliche Werke*, part II, vol. 9 (*Johannes*), 269-70.

request in response to the silent prayer of his heart, which he knew for a certainty had been heard before he spoke it aloud.[34]

Jesus' perfect God-consciousness means that each of his thoughts is a prayer, and every prayer is granted because it is in accordance with the divine will. Thus, Schleiermacher affirms the miracle of the raising of Lazarus, and he goes on to comment on miracle as a ground for faith. Some who saw the raising of Lazarus came to believe in Christ, but others did not. At the very best, miracles are a secondary basis for belief. They are simply works of God, like any other act or creature whose origin is in God. Our acceptance of them as part of belief depends on the disposition of our minds. Those who saw the raising of Lazarus and came to believe in Christ were those who were already disposed toward belief. Even the most wonderful and extraordinary act of Christ could convince only those who in their inner disposition were already prepared for belief. This is in accordance with Schleiermacher's discussion in *The Christian Faith*, where he remarks that faith can be produced without miracles, and that miracles often fail to produce faith in those who witness them:

> Since, in connection with the divine revelation in Christ, phenomena presented themselves which could be brought under this concept of miracle, it was natural that they should be . . . adduced as confirmation of the fact that this was a new point of development. But this confirmation will be effectual only where there is present a beginning of faith.[35]

Thus, faith does not rest upon miracles; belief in miracles is a product of faith. Faith cannot be compelled, but arises spontaneously from recognition of the unity of the Redeemer with our Father in heaven.

THE RESURRECTION OF CHRIST

The question of Schleiermacher's attitude to the resurrection may serve as a summary and conclusion to the question of the historical nature of the Gospels. It is frequently supposed that he denied the fact of the resurrection, but this must be regarded as mistaken. Schleiermacher objected to the way in which the resurrection was used for doctrinal purposes, as if knowledge of the resurrection could compel faith. He therefore sought to separate the fact of the resurrection from the doctrine of Christ's person, and his own attitude to the historical question was seldom more than hinted at in the

---

34. *Saemmtliche Werke*, part II, vol. 9 (*Johannes*), 278–79.
35. *Christian Faith*, vol. 1 (14), 72–73.

writings which are generally known. However, even in *The Christian Faith* there are suggestions which should prevent hasty judgments on the matter.

In *The Christian Faith*, Schleiermacher denies that the fact of the resurrection has any significance for the doctrine of Christ's person. This is in accordance with his principle that nothing can be set up as a real doctrine with respect to him, "unless it is connected with his redeeming causality and can be traced to the original impression made by his existence."[36] The being of God in Christ is the basis both for his redemptive work and for the impression of him, which is the ground of faith. None of this depends on any particular fact such as the resurrection. Neither for the original disciples, nor for those who have come to belief at a subsequent time, was this either the unique or the sufficient ground of faith. In this regard, Schleiermacher seems to be reflecting on his own life and giving an indication of his own personal history: he did not come to a belief in Christ because he had been convinced about the resurrection, but rather, he was convinced by the total impression of Christ, and on that basis formed his opinion of the resurrection.

Knowledge of the resurrection is not, for Schleiermacher, a prerequisite of faith. The disciples came to believe in Christ before they had any idea of this event; his influence upon subsequent generations is quite independent of any certainty about it. Paul refers to Christ's resurrection as the guarantee of the belief among Christians in their own resurrection, and in this way, he does link it with Christ's redeeming work—but even Paul does not refer to the matter as an integral part of the doctrine of Christ's person. Hence, Schleiermacher concludes that a right impression of Christ can be formed and maintained without any affirmation of the fact of the resurrection. This is in line with Schleiermacher's general principle of hermeneutics: the general impression which is the basis of interpretation cannot rest on any one fact whatsoever, or even on a group of facts; it is an impression of the whole which is partially present in each individual event, but not dependent upon any of them. No one fact about the life of Christ can be decisive for our view of his person, not even the resurrection. Similarly, we can see here the reflection of Schleiermacher's view of religion as the feeling of absolute dependence: religion as feeling is independent of knowledge. Knowledge is separate from and irrelevant to religious feeling, and therefore Christianity cannot be based on knowledge of the fact of the resurrection.

The resurrection is therefore independent of the doctrine of Christ and ought not to be a part of the creed about him. It is not, however, independent

---

36. *Christian Faith*, vol. 1 (29:3), 125. For this section, see *The Christian Faith*, vol. 1 (99:1), 417–19.

of our doctrine of Scripture, nor of our actual practice of interpreting Scripture.[37] As part of the exegesis of Scripture, our view of the resurrection may reflect indirectly on our doctrine of Christ. If the disciples were stupid and unreliable so that they reported as fact things which had not taken place, then Christ, who chose such followers, did not deserve the dignity which is ascribed to him within the church. A similar conclusion would result if the resurrection was regarded as a fraud in which Christ himself connived. Therefore, our attitude to the resurrection must be based on our judgment of the Gospels as reports of events, and of their authors as reporters.

Schleiermacher's own judgment of the matter is well buried in the mass of his writings. In *Introduction to the New Testament*,[38] there is a section dealing with the resurrection stories in the Synoptic Gospels, and also a number of paragraphs dealing with the accounts in John. An examination of the various accounts leads Schleiermacher to conclude that the records of the resurrection in the Synoptics are a collection of disconnected tales which are entirely lacking in chronological sequence, and which have been put together in an arbitrary manner at a later time. They make it impossible to regard any unified account of the resurrection as being an integral part of the original apostolic preaching. But they do show clearly that the apostles designated themselves as witnesses to the resurrection. Their primary motive in doing so was to establish the fact that the death of Christ had not hindered the coming establishment of the kingdom of God. Belief in the resurrection has existed in the church as long as there has been belief in Christ:

> It is clear that the fact of the resurrection has been believed from the beginning. Thus, the stories about it can in no way be dismissed as deception. If one believes in the honesty of the reporter, one must also believe in the fact. There is no evidence of any doubt about the resurrection of Christ earlier than that in the Corinthian congregation.[39]

The accounts of the resurrection display characteristics similar to those in other parts of the various Gospels. Matthew's Gospel recounts stories for which there can have been no reliable basis, and which cannot be combined in a coherent account. Much of its material is an imaginary filling out of the story with impossible details. Mark is dismissed with a brief comment that the promise to appear in Galilee is recorded but not fulfilled. On the other hand, Luke's Gospel gives a clear and coherent account of how news

---

37. *Christian Faith*, vol. 2 (99:2), 419–21.
38. *Saemmtliche Werke*, part I, vol. 8 (*Neue Testament*), 295–302.
39. *Saemmtliche Werke*, part I, vol. 8 (*Neue Testament*), 297.

of the resurrection first came to the disciples. It is an account which can be easily combined with that in John's Gospel. The most important section of Luke's account is the story of Christ's appearance on the road to Emmaus. The purpose of this appearance is that Christ may give an explanation of his messiahship in relation to the events of the crucifixion, and the editor of the gospel has taken care to see that it is not interpreted as the appearance of a nonmaterial spirit. It is John's Gospel which gives the best account: it has a better idea of the timing of the appearance, and its stories bear the characteristics of eyewitness reports. The empty tomb is not the important circumstance of the resurrection: that might have been explained by saying that Christ's body was given temporary burial on the Sabbath, and had already been removed for more permanent disposition, by Joseph of Arimathea, before the woman came in the morning. But Schleiermacher accepts as reliable the accounts in John's Gospel of Christ's appearances on the two occasions in Jerusalem and the third time in Galilee: "Here the stories are of a kind that show the characteristics of an eye-witness account, and in part they indicate direct personal participation."[40] In this way, Schleiermacher accepted the resurrection of Christ as fact, but he interpreted the fact in an unusual way. He did not regard the period of the resurrection as a continuous period of fellowship between Christ and the disciples. Instead, he thought that there was a series of disconnected appearances to various people at various times.

In a sermon on the resurrection, Schleiermacher went beyond the bare fact of resurrection to affirm the connection of new life to the old:

> He was the same and was recognized by His disciples as the same, to their great joy; His whole appearance was the very same; even in the glory of His resurrection He bore the marks of His wounds as a remembrance of His sufferings and as the tokens of His death; and the remembrance of His former state was most closely and constantly with Him.... The resurrection of the Lord was no new creation, but the same Man, Jesus, who had gone down into the grave, came forth again from it.[41]

The fact of the resurrection has no significance for the person of Christ, but it is the basis for our belief in the resurrection of the flesh. Christ's resurrection is the indication to us of how our new life may resemble the present life. But ideas of a future life are mere hints and cannot be made definite.

---

40. *Saemmtliche Werke*, part I, vol. 8 (*Neue Testament*), 330–31.
41. *Saemmtliche Werke*, part II, vol. 2 (*Vierte-Siebente Sammlung*), 180; *Selected Sermons*, 270.

Schleiermacher's interpretation of the resurrection appearances is consistent with his attitude toward other incidents in the Gospels. Judgment of the historical nature of the reports must be kept separate from the evaluation of its position in dogmatic teaching. Doctrine cannot depend on particular facts for authentication, but rests on a total impression: the resurrection as a fact is not a dogmatic requirement. For this reason, Schleiermacher, in most of his writing, refrained from declaring his own judgment about the fact. But it cannot be denied that he considered the general question of historical authenticity as very important, and judged the gospel picture of Christ as reliable. In the end, he also affirmed the fact of the resurrection of Christ, and its significance for the Christian hope.

5

The Use of the Old Testament

LITTLE IS MORE PERSISTENT in Schleiermacher's writings than his rejection of the Old Testament as a source for Christianity. In the development of his thought on dogmatics and ethics in his major works, his essays, and his sermons, there is a recurring contrast of Old Testament and New Testament, law and gospel, Christianity and Judaism. The extent of his rejection of Jewish thought is shocking to an age that has learned to be defensive about anything appearing to be anti-Semitic. British puritanism is the source of a tendency in English-language theological thought to transfer Old Testament texts directly to a Christian setting, but Schleiermacher owed nothing to this tradition and proceeded in an opposite direction. In German theology, the stress upon justification by faith in Reformed and Lutheran orthodoxy had guarded against a rigid concept of law, and because the Old Testament was regarded as fulfilled in Christ, it was regarded as much less important than the New Testament for Christian theology. However, in his depreciation of the Old Testament, Schleiermacher went far beyond the orthodox tradition.

In his *Addresses on Religion*, Schleiermacher outlined a harsh position with regard to Judaism, and his later writings give no evidence of any subsequent softening of his position:

> Perhaps I should speak of just one particular religion: for Judaism has long been a dead faith, and those who now wear its colours sit wailing before the undecaying mummy and weep

> over its demise and its sad legacy. I speak of it not because it is somehow the fore-runner of Christianity: I hate this kind of historical reference in religion. The necessity of religion is something higher and more eternal, and each beginning in religion is something original. But Judaism had such a wonderfully childish character, and this has been so completely overwhelmed, and the whole has become a remarkable example of corruption and of the complete disappearance of the great substance of religion which formerly existed in it.[1]

The character of Judaism is the character displayed by the Old Testament:

> What is the idea of the Universal which underlies it throughout? No other than that of general and immediate retaliation, of a particular reaction against every capricious act of the finite individual through the act of another finite individual which is regarded as uncapricious. . . . All other attributes of God are expressed according to this rule, and are seen in relationship to it: rewarding, punishing, disciplining the individual through individuals.[2]

In this chapter, the development of Schleiermacher's concept of the Old Testament will be followed in his later writings. Relevant sections of *The Christian Faith* are considered in detail, but attention is also given to certain sermons, *Die christliche Sittenlehre*, and some other writings.

THE CHRISTIAN FAITH

Schleiermacher deals with the Old Testament principally in three sections of *The Christian Faith*. In the first, his discussion is part of his comment on the relationship of Christianity to Judaism.[3] Judaism provided the historical setting in which Jesus was born, but it has no other particular significance. Jewish religion was monotheistic, and hence was a proper source for one who was to be the Universal Redeemer, but Schleiermacher warns against giving this factor an undue emphasis. Jewish culture was monotheistic but contained many elements of alien origin, and many of its prophetic elements were ignored in Jesus' day. On the other hand, Greek and Roman thought, while polytheistic, contained many elements which were tending toward monotheism.

---

1. *Ueber die Religion*, 286-87.
2. *Ueber die Religion*, 287-88.
3. *Christian Faith*, vol. 1 (12:1), 60; see also (8:4) 37-38; (12:3) 62.

Thus, for Schleiermacher, Judaism was no more essential as a background for Christianity than Greek thought. In fact, both provided the historical setting for Christianity, the former as the setting for Jesus' birth, the latter as the culture which provided the bulk of the converts to Christianity.

Thus, Judaism is regarded merely from the point of view of the history of religions. In this connection, Schleiermacher had some curious notions. Judaism was a Mosaic institution developed by the prophets. Mesopotamian influences on Hebrew thought were subsequent to this pure Judaism, absorbed during and after the dispersion by the Babylonians. Schleiermacher does not seem to have had any inkling of the deep roots of Judaism in the ancient myths of the Fertile Crescent. The archeological discoveries which laid the basis of modern study of comparative religion were subsequent to Schleiermacher's writing, but they substantially disproved his conceptions of the relationship of the Old Testament to the religious thought of neighboring peoples.

As a world religion, Schleiermacher refers to Judaism as one of the three great monotheistic communions, along with Christianity and Islam. He gives no particular significance to the fact that both Christianity and Islam have deep historical and spiritual roots in Judaism. They are simply three separate religions of the monotheistic type, each with its own characteristics and tendencies. Christianity is regarded as the highest of the three because of the tendency to fetish worship in early Judaism and the sensuous content of Muslim worship.

Both Christianity and Islam, in Schleiermacher's view, are contending for the mastery of the human race. On the other hand, the Jewish religion is declining, in danger of extinction. With such a view of Judaism, it is scarcely surprising that Schleiermacher depreciates the Old Testament. The Mosaic law is part of the divine economy only in the same sense as Greek philosophy: both Old Testament sayings and heathen messianic prophecies are an expression of the striving of human nature toward Christianity. In another section, Schleiermacher evaluates the Old Testament for dogmatic work.[4] His conclusion is both emphatic and clear: "The Old Testament appears simply a superfluous authority for Dogmatics."[5]

All doctrines accepted within the teaching of the evangelical churches must be based either directly or indirectly upon the New Testament. Human claims are only useful for supporting doctrine if they are attested by Scripture. The use to which Scripture is put may vary widely because of the free application of linguistic criticism to biblical exegesis. Moreover, it

---

4. *Christian Faith*, vol. 1 (27:3), 115–16.
5. *Christian Faith*, vol. 1 (27:3), 115.

is important that, in eliciting doctrines from the Bible, a large-viewed approach be used, so that the general sense of large passages and numbers of books be included in the doctrine, rather than the apparent meaning of a particular verse. Schleiermacher is arguing indirectly against the use of prooftexts, a practice particularly dear to the theologians of the reformed churches in the age of Protestant scholasticism. On this point, he is urging a change in emphasis from the course followed by dogmatic theology up to his day. But on the relation of the two parts of the Bible to one another, he is advocating revolution: appeal to the Scriptures means appeal to the New Testament alone:

> If a doctrine had neither direct nor indirect attestation in the New Testament, but only in the Old, no one could have much confidence in regarding it as a genuinely Christian doctrine: whereas if a doctrine is attested by the New Testament, no one will object to it, because there is nothing about it in the Old.[6]

In a third section of *The Christian Faith*,[7] Schleiermacher bases his discussion of the Old Testament on the consideration of the Jewish law. In his view, law and gospel are antithetical one toward another. The Christian life must flow from the power of the Spirit; but the law lacks this Spirit. For corroboration, he refers to Galatians 3:2: "Did you receive the Spirit by doing the works of the law or by believing what you heard?" (NRSV).

Schleiermacher's interpretation of this differs from the tradition of reformed theology: God sends the Spirit into men's hearts solely through the work of Christ, and in no sense through the law. The Spirit is an entirely new gift given subsequent to the crucifixion, and in no sense is it the return of something which had been given in former times. It is this concept of the work of the Holy Spirit which is the key to Schleiermacher's rejection of the Old Testament, and which gives rise to his sharpest expression. The Holy Spirit is the common spirit alive in the consciousness of the Christian community. The common spirit among Christians is different from the general ethos of Judaism and the Old Testament. Hence, for Schleiermacher, it is a mistake to speak of the work of the Holy Spirit prior to Pentecost; the Holy Spirit is not to be seen in the Old Testament, or even in the early sections of the New Testament. The consequence is that the Old Testament is seen as proceeding from a spirit different from that of the New Testament, a spirit which is contrary to the Holy Spirit known among Christians. Only the fact that Christ himself and the early disciples used the Old Testament for their

---

6. *Christian Faith*, vol. 1 (27:3), 115.
7. *Christian Faith*, vol. 2 (132:2), 608–10; see also (132:3) 610–11.

teaching prevents Schleiermacher from fully rejecting its place in the Bible, as Marcion had done.

Because the Old Testament law is rejected, prophecy must also be rejected. Both history and prophecy in the Old Testament, in Schleiermacher's view, are subsequent to and dependent upon the legal dispensation. The historical books merely provide the setting for the giving of the law, and as the law is superseded, the history is rendered irrelevant. The prophetical books are concerned, for the most part, with matters of law, and it is only on the question of messianic prophecy that they could make any claim whatsoever to inspiration. Yet messianic prophecy is a very isolated occurrence in the writings of the prophets, and such occurrences can best be regarded as evidence of the common spirit of man rising to a consciousness of the need of redemption. This can be regarded as the work of the Holy Spirit only in the sense that it constitutes a premonition of an inward and spiritual reign of God, and thus a preparation and a condition for the gift of the Holy Spirit. It is inspiration only in a secondary sense of that term. Thus, prophecy fares little better than history, in Schleiermacher's view.

As a source of piety, the Old Testament has no great value. Whenever its texts are used for the expressing of pious feeling, there is usually an accompanying style of thought which is legalistic and slavish in worshipping the letter. Thus, the Psalms may not be used as Christian praise without conscious or unconscious additions and subtractions from the sentiments of the writers, even of the noblest passages. Christian piety can never rely unreservedly upon such passages, or similar ones in the prophetic books, without reference to the New Testament. Even to the extent that they contain premonitions of the doctrine of redemption, they are useless when placed beside the words of Christ and the experience of his disciples. The doctrine of redemption in the Old Testament should not be overemphasized, because if it had really been so important, the reception which Jesus received from those of his contemporaries who knew their Bible would have been far different from what it was.

The place which the Old Testament held in the life of the church depends in the first place on historical grounds. Christ and the disciples followed the practice of reading passages from it and then commenting upon them, a practice which was perpetuated in the life of the church. But with the formation of the canon of the New Testament, it was right and proper that the Old should recede into the background. The way in which this should occur is illustrated by the use which Paul makes of the Old Testament: his interpretation is very free, to the extent that one can say that proofs from it are no longer required. The history of Christian theology supports this point of view: the effort to find Christian doctrine within the Old Testament has been a great detriment to the practice of exegesis, leading to unnecessary controversy and submerging the development of doctrinal definition under a flood of useless complications. Schleiermacher maintained that this deleterious effect would end only when the Old Testament was discarded for doctrinal purposes.

The second basis on which the Christian use of the books of the Old Testament depended was that Christ and the apostles themselves referred to the Old Testament as a divine authority. For reasons of historical fidelity, the church needs to preserve the books which they quoted, chiefly the Psalms and the prophetic books. The fact that some quotations occur from other books, and that in Jesus' day the collection of the various books into the Old Testament canon had been made, is reason enough for retaining the whole. But, on this basis, it is still only those parts which are quoted in the New Testament which retain any authority. Therefore, Schleiermacher rejects the notion that the study of the Old Testament is the proper method of approach to the theology of the New Testament. To emphasize this point, he said that he would prefer to see the Old Testament printed as an appendix to the New, rather than as a prior and equal partner with it.

Schleiermacher's fundamental basis for rejecting the Old Testament is the logical development of his whole approach to theology: the actual experience of the religious consciousness. What is the need for ancient premonitions of faith in the face of the witness of experience? The witness of ancient authority is properly discarded when men and women can gain an immediate certainty through their own perception. Schleiermacher refers to John's Gospel in support of this position:

> And many more believed because of his word. They said to the woman, "It is no longer because of what you said that we believe, for we have heard for ourselves, and we know that this is truly the Savior of the world." (John 4:41–42 NRSV)

Religion is feeling, and feeling is a constituent of the human self-consciousness. Experience and perception are the proper bases of the self-consciousness, and anything which is learned by way of reflection or intellectual process is only of secondary importance in questions of religion. Thus, in Schleiermacher's view, a documentary source is a poor substitute for the direct awareness of the feeling of absolute dependence. If this argument is sufficient to demolish the authority of the Old Testament, it is hard to see why it should not apply with equal force to the New. The text quoted from John is one which relegates indirect witness to the direct words of Jesus himself. There is no reason why the indirect witness should be identified with the Old Testament; it can be applied with equal validity to the writings of Paul or those of Luke, although Schleiermacher does not, in fact, do so. He still retains the New Testament as authoritative for Christian piety and doctrine:

> The individual books of the New Testament are inspired by the Holy Spirit, and the collection of them took place under the guidance of the Holy Spirit.[8]

In principle, it is hard to see how the criticism applied to one part of the Bible may not also be applied to the other, and subsequent writers were quick to proceed in this way.

CREATION

The general position of *The Christian Faith* with respect to the Old Testament is thus very negative, and its position with regard to particular doctrines in the Old Testament is equally negative. Two aspects of Christian teaching which have relied heavily on the Old Testament for material are ethics and the doctrine of creation. Both are treated in *The Christian Faith* in a way which illustrates this negative approach, and other works are similar in tendency. In *The Christian Faith*, Schleiermacher begins his consideration of the doctrine of creation by drawing a distinction between its position in the teaching of the New Testament and that of the Old.[9] In the Old Testament, creation is set out as the beginning of a history book, and its purpose is to supply knowledge. In setting forth the Christian doctrine, Schleiermacher's aim is to prevent any suggestion of a knowledge of origins, which he would regard as material that is alien to piety. It is not, in his opinion, the purpose of the New Testament to satisfy curiosity. The religious interest lies in the development of feeling, and interest in a doctrine such as creation is only indirect. Thus, the section dealing with creation is headed by references only to the New Testament, accompanied by the comment that they are essentially negative in character and prevent any closer definition or more definite conception. Exact definitions of creation are an intrusion into dogmatics which come from a time when the Bible was used as a textbook for natural science. Now that natural science has developed its own methods of research, further investigation of the origins of the world may be left in its hands, without any dependence upon Christian doctrine, either in its procedure or in its results.

---

8. *Christian Faith*, vol. 2 (130), 597.
9. *Christian Faith* vol. 1 (39:1), 148–49, (39:2), 149.

These remarks are the starting point for Schleiermacher's consideration of the opening chapters of Genesis.[10] He denies that they have any genuine historical character. His first ground for this is the diverse character of the creation stories in the first and second chapters. In addition, other Old Testament passages, together with New Testament and early commentators, interpreted the passages very freely or very simply. Even if it could be established that the Genesis accounts were historical, they would still not be a part of doctrine, since they would merely be an addition to our information, but not to our feeling of absolute dependence; it is the feeling of absolute dependence which is the basis of doctrine. The narrative passages of Genesis are characterized as myth. They belong to a period prior to the growth of abstract scientific speculation, which Schleiermacher characterizes as primitive and prehistoric. As such, in his view, they do not have any particular religious or Christian character. He regards this interpretation of the early parts of Genesis as consistent with many passages in the Old Testament itself, which handled the Genesis accounts very freely, and with an early postbiblical interpretation of them. His conclusion is that literal interpretation was never universally prevalent and that there is no requirement for Christian theology to hold a literal interpretation. Without any detailed discussion, he indicates that he dismisses the notion of the days of creation, the story of the garden of Eden, and the early accounts of the patriarchs.

In Schleiermacher's view, the purpose of the doctrine of creation is a negative one: it guards against the idea that anything can have an origin other than in God. He regards this as a support for his idea of God as the source of our idea of absolute dependence: absolute dependence excludes origination of anything in a source other than God. He regards creation as a doctrine equivalent to the doctrine of the preservation of all things in God. Both mean the dependence of the totality of finite being upon the infinite, and therefore the dependence of ourselves as finite beings apart from other things, and the dependence of every other finite existence, including the world itself. Creation deals with this dependence in terms of absolute beginning, but if it is considered in isolation, it excludes the idea of development, which is conjoined to it in our consciousness. Thus, the idea of preservation must be maintained in the closest possible connection with the idea of creation. Preservation is the doctrine which continues the idea of dependence through time, allowing for development in the world and hence for our consciousness of continuous existence in the past, present, and future. Both

---

10. *Christian Faith*, vol. 1 (40:1), 150; (40:2) 150–51. For this section, see also (36:1) 142–43, (36:2) 143, (39) 148–49, (40) 149–52.

doctrines together express the absolute dependence of the natural world upon God, and of the ordering of all in a system of natural interdependence.

An interesting sidelight on the doctrine of creation is provided by a sermon which Schleiermacher preached at the New Year between 1823 and 1826.[11] It is based on Job 38:11: "Thus, far shall you come, and no farther, and here shall your proud waves be stayed."

The interpretation of creation in this sermon provides a contrast to the discussion found in *The Christian Faith*. Creation is here regarded as the establishment of order. God is he who has called everything into being, who sustains everything by his word, and he is also the one who has given to everything in the world its limits and its order. Nothing can resist his word of power, nor can anything extend itself beyond the limits which he has imposed on it.

This general thesis is applied successively to a consideration of creation, of the world of nature, of general human affairs, of human knowledge, and of the life of the church, which in this sermon is seen as God's new creation. The original creation was the forming of the world at the call of God, in which he divided and united all things. Each created thing is limited, as it is made by the creation of its opposite. The work of creation was the separation of light and darkness, solid and liquid, so that each would have its place and be of advantage to the other. Thus, the order of nature is established—and the world is enabled to support life—through the mixing and limiting of various natural forces. Natural life is a constant recurrence of destruction and rebuilding, but all in one direction, so that from the seeming destruction, a better order of things results. The limits placed upon the destructive forces are imposed by God, who uses these forces for the ordering of the world. Against the power of nature, man's feeling of powerlessness is awakened, and the stilling of the storm makes men turn to the Lord, from whom comes order and limitation in the world.

A similar situation prevails in human affairs; the natural world in this respect is a reflection of the spiritual world. God has created man by breathing life into him and making a rational soul. Man's order and his limit are provided by his reason and his moral sense, and despite the destructive power of human life, God maintains this limit so that reason and morality are not utterly subverted, but are sustained against the forces of destruction by a power which God has established in human nature. Within intellectual life itself, a similar balance is maintained, so that those who believe that they have discovered the secret of everything, and seek to use it to control life, are

---

11. *Saemmtliche Werke*, part II, vol. 2 (*Vierte-Siebente Sammlung*), 85–103; *Selected Sermons*, 212.

faced with new problems which destroy their preconceived solutions. They are then forced to admit their powerlessness and to acknowledge the order which is established by the creator.

The Christian church is God's new creation, formed as God sent his only begotten Son as the Word made flesh. The new creation is a creation in the hearts of men by the Spirit of God, in which we await the new heaven and new earth. In the new creation, as in the old, the significant things are order and limits. Within the church, human ambition and striving continue (and from earliest times have led to unfaithfulness and disobedience), but in the end, the Spirit has established the limits of destruction with the word of peace. The rule of the Spirit within the church is a sign and a warning for Christians to heed Christ's statement: "My kingdom is not of this world." The progress of the church is the task of freeing it from bondage to human considerations—and for the use of all its gifts for the common building of the work of the Spirit. Thus, all creation is a work of ordering, and in Schleiermacher's view, it is not complete. The new creation is a further extension of the old creation, a creation of Spirit rather than of nature. Christ has a part in the work of creation, and the task of the church is to carry out Christ's work of order in obedience to the Spirit.

This sermon carries Schleiermacher's exposition of creation far beyond the narrow position established in *The Christian Faith*. In the sermon, he does not make any comparison between the accounts of creation in Genesis and Job. He does not regard Job as having any special authority, referring to the passage as "a sublime discourse which is put by the writer in the mouth of the highest Being, the creator and preserver of the world." Job is an ancient holy book which ascribes certain sayings to God. Thus, Job is given no higher position than the accounts in Genesis, and Schleiermacher does not seek to use Job as a necessary basis for doctrine. As in his dogmatic thought, the doctrine of creation is brought into close connection with concepts of preservation, development, and order. However, the sermon gives greater emphasis to the continuous creative activity of God and to the place of Christ in the work of creation. Although not contradictory to the doctrinal exposition, the sermon has a fresh approach which is more positive in its attitude toward continuity between the Old and New Testaments.

ETHICS

Reference has already been made to Schleiermacher's rejection of the Jewish law as part of his general consideration of the authority and importance of the Old Testament. A similar rejection occurs in Schleiermacher's discussions of good works and moral conduct. In *The Christian Faith*, he discusses good works and the use of the law, with particular reference to Lutheran confessional statements.[12] In the *Formula of Concord*, three uses of the law are set forth:

i. The law is used to maintain outward discipline and honesty in opposition to unruly and disobedient people.

ii. The law is used so that sinners may be brought to a knowledge of their sin.

iii. In addition, for those who are reborn through the Spirit of God, who have been converted unto the Lord, and who are clothed already in the garments of Moses, the law is taught so that they may live and walk in true piety.[13]

Schleiermacher, in rejecting the second and third of these uses of the law, rejects the substantial tradition of both Lutheran and Reformed theology concerning the basis of moral teaching. He does not reject the first use of the law: he admits that even in Christian life there will exist some kind of legislation, with regulations concerning arts and crafts which act as a guide for those who are lacking in insight; and this civil law is a good work if based on love, and even a means of grace because it involves our spiritual powers. Schleiermacher, in common with the traditional Protestant interpreters, gives this regulative use of the law no value in producing sanctification. The penal use of the law he rejects as inadequate, for sin can only be displayed for what it is by a comparison with Christ; law can show only the outward discrepancy and not the inward one. It is the third use of the law which he rejects most decidedly, because the law can never show us the strength and purity of inward disposition, which is the goal of sanctification. Hence, Schleiermacher rejects the use of the Decalogue either as a means of awakening people to a sense of sin, or as a means of instruction in good works. He regards its use in this way as an invitation to bad, arbitrary exegesis, leading to an imperfect and superficial conception of Christian behavior.

The law is not done away with because Christ has fulfilled it.[14] Such a conception is improper, in Schleiermacher's view. The very existence of a law implies a separation between a will which ordains the law and the will which conforms to the law; the former may be perfect, but the latter must

---

12. *Christian Faith* vol. 2 (112:5), 523. See also vol. 1 (70:3), 284–85; vol. 2 (144:1), 660–61.

13. Lietzmann, *Bekenntnisschriften*, 962.

14. *Christian Faith*, vol. 2 (104:3), 453–57. See notes 22 and 23 below for contradictory references.

be imperfect and subordinate. Thus, Christ cannot, in any sense, have been subject to the law, either as an enforced subjection or by a willing submission. Christ's obedience is given not to a divine law, but to the divine will, and the concept of perfect obedience to law as a factor in man's redemption is rejected. Christ's action on our behalf is to free us from the law; the same action which frees us from sin also frees us from the law. As a result of these considerations, in *The Christian Faith*, Schleiermacher's conclusion is that Christian ethics will be most truly expounded, and stand in the proper relationship to dogmatics, if it avoids the conception of commandments and the category of law altogether.

This conclusion is echoed in his other works. The understanding of ethics as obedience to an imperative, in Schleiermacher's view, belongs to a stage of moral development which had not yet learned to distinguish between ethics and politics. In his discussion in *The Difference between Natural Law and Moral Law*, he classifies the Old Testament law as belonging to such a primitive stage of human development:

> In the prescriptions of the Jewish law the concerns of universal humanity were mixed up with particular considerations of civil law and religious practice, and all were ascribed to theocratic authorship. This was necessary because the climate of opinion in which the people had lived for so long was one which had entirely suppressed the sense of universal human concern, and which made necessary a denial that everything might be permitted.[15]

Schleiermacher's principal criticism of every imperative system of ethics centers itself in the claim that in it, the moral realm is thought of as nonexistent. In contrast, he calls for a realism in morality which takes account of the actual circumstances in which men lived:

> The presentation of Christian ethics cannot always be the same, as a different one is needed and possible in various periods. Thus, there may be an exposition of Christian teaching for the present, but certainly not one which is valid for all time.[16]

In his lectures on Christian ethics, Schleiermacher is just as suspicious of the use of the Old Testament as a basis of Christian teaching as he is in *The Christian Faith*. He again names the Scriptures as the original charter of Christianity, in that it is a confirmation of the content of the original Christian consciousness. But for ethics, the Old Testament is entirely discarded:

15. *Saemmtliche Werke*, part III, vol. 2 (*Ueber den Unterschied*), 404.
16. *Saemmtliche Werke*, part I, vol. 12 (*Die christliche Sitte*), 9.

in Schleiermacher's opinion, to disregard the difference between the two sections of the Bible is even more dangerous for Christian ethics than for doctrine, because the use of the Decalogue introduces a systematic legal spirit into ethics.[17]

Christian ethics is descriptive, not prescriptive, and its task is to describe those patterns of behavior which arise out of a religious self-consciousness which is Christian in character. Because of the divine Spirit which is determinative of Christian life, it is possible to ignore any distinction between obligation and act. Love is put in place of law, and becomes increasingly the effective impulse of behavior. It is the living force of faith, and it determines the reality of the rule of God and all inner development of human consciousness. For this reason, ethics may dispense with obligation and allow description of actual life in the church to take its place. The rejection of Mosaic commandments is only part of an extended polemic against all imperative forms of ethical teaching.

In his sermons, Schleiermacher outlines a motive for Christian conduct which is quite different from that of Jewish piety. In the Old Testament, there is a pattern of action and reaction in which human behavior earns God's approval or disapproval. God's will is seen as arbitrary, and piety is seen as obedience to law. The law stands over against men, promising or threatening punishment, so that hope and fear are the correlative motives of conduct. In a previous section, it has been noted that Schleiermacher considers the contrast between law and gospel as the key to Paul's theology. Two of the sermons on the Augsburg Confession, based on Galatians 2, deal with the subject.[18] Another sermon, an Advent address (based on Galatians 3:21–23) from an earlier period, rejects law as a source for Christian conduct and sets Christ forth as the one who sets us free from sin and from law:

> Sin and the law hang together so closely, that the one cannot be thought of without the other, and the one can be taken away only by an act which also removes the other. A divine act which can really make us holy cannot make peace either with the consciousness of sin or with a law.[19]

Law is seen as a concern of man's understanding, whether law is conceived of as a gift of divine revelation or as a product of merely human reflection. In the latter case, it is obviously the product of the human understanding which chooses precepts and determines limits. But even a divine

17. *Saemmtliche Werke*, part I, vol. 12 (*Die christliche Sitte*), 167. Manuscript of 1828.

18. See also ch. 3, "Interpreting Pauline Doctrine."

19. *Saemmtliche Werke*, part II, vol. 2 (*Vierte-Siebente Sammlung*), 29.

law is formulated in words and is impressed upon humanity by means of speech—and thus it too concerns their intellectual faculty. Obedience to law, however, is a matter of the will, and human will does not always follow the guidance of understanding. This conflict of understanding and will, Schleiermacher maintains, is the reason sin and law are always found to be together, and are equally burdensome to the human conscience. In a law like the Jewish law, conceived of as a revelation of God, a great mass of burdensome outward customs is mixed up with precepts which are inward and spiritual in content and concern the relations of human to human and human to God. They are set out in such a way that the one is as important as the other, and thus the law itself becomes a burden which men long to discard along with sin, which signifies their inability even to come near to a perfect obedience. But even a more rational law of human devising has a similar defect, because of the division between the understanding and the will. Thus, there never has been a law, nor can there be, such as would give life. Christ gives us life by setting us free from law, and this is the same as redeeming us from sin. He is able to do this because for him the division between understanding and will does not exist. Christ is therefore not subject to the law, and likewise is free from sin. Christians are given a share in Christ's righteousness, and in their lives, the division of understanding and will is overcome, making them strangers both to sin and the law. Freedom, for the Christian, is to be redeemed from the law and from sin, and to be drawn through faith into unity of life with Christ.

In another sermon, the motive of Christian conduct is contrasted with that of behavior under the old covenant:

> The law was given to believers in the old covenant] as an established letter which obligated them to outward obedience. Reward and blessing was offered to them on the one side, curse and punishment on the other. The whole law was merely a shadow of the sanctifying will of God. The substance of this will is that we must bear the word of God written in indelible letters in our innermost being, within our whole disposition, in the depth of our hearts, so that the will of God becomes our own will, and His law the law of our own life.[20]

In our new life in Christ, his relationship to the Father is formed in us, so that we become sons of God, sharing the power that is in Christ. This conception of the Christian life is peculiarly a Protestant view, and Schleiermacher, in his sermons (as in his teaching on doctrine and ethics), draws a sharp line between Protestant and Roman Catholic interpretation.

20. *Saemmtliche Werke*, part II, vol. 2 (*Vierte-Siebente Sammlung*), 507–8.

A continued emphasis on ceremonial spirit and the inculcation of a legal one are, to his mind, continuing marks of Roman Catholic teaching:

> Has not a permanent separation taken place within the church because one section of Christendom chose to retain those elements which preserved the fearful spirit of the outward legalism of the Old Testament, which borrowed the glittering pomp of sensuous paganism, and which endangered the equality of all under the one master?[21]

Schleiermacher's rejection of the Old Testament is nowhere more plain than in his discussion of ethics. His philosophical legacy from Kant is evident in this aspect of his system, and he points forward to the development of ethics as the description of behavior.

SUMMARY

The general position discernible in all these examples of Schleiermacher's writing is a sharp rejection of the Old Testament for all purposes within the Christian church. In his own work, he cites the Old Testament infrequently. Of the 220 sermons in the collections published during Schleiermacher's lifetime, only twelve are on Old Testament texts. None of them are based on the Pentateuch, and only two are on the latter prophets; nine are on texts from the poetical writings. *The Christian Faith* has fewer references to the Old Testament than to Romans, and many of these references, the greatest number being to Genesis, are explanations of why the Old Testament should not be freely used in the church. It is remarkable that Schleiermacher felt able to adopt such a negative attitude to the Old Testament and yet maintain that his system of doctrine was based on the general consciousness of the church. He is accused in many quarters of retaining in his system only those ideas which could be deduced from his philosophical principles, and of disallowing all other traditional formulations. This charge is an exaggeration, because he retained elements of the teaching of Christ and the church's teaching of Christ's person which fitted badly with his philosophical presuppositions. But the Old Testament received harsher treatment. Nothing in it survived his critical attack, and even parts which Schleiermacher considered sublime in their spirit were not admitted to positions of authority in his system.

---

21. *Saemmtliche Werke*, part II, vol. 2 (*Vierte-Siebente Sammlung*), 93; *Selected Sermons*, 222.

A number of problems remain to disturb the consistency of Schleiermacher's position, and may be considered together under the heading of fulfilment. There is a sense in which Schleiermacher regards the New Testament as the fulfilment of the Old. In his *Introduction to the New Testament* he states:

> As Christians we must not confuse the characteristics of the time of promise and those of the time of fulfilment, and we must maintain the course adopted by the New Testament. In bringing together the fulfilment of the divine promises in Christ the New Testament establishes that it gives the first light concerning the decrees of God, and anything previous to him is only a hint. There remains the essential difference between the kingdom of God as preached by Jesus and his disciples, and the prospect of such a kingdom previously hinted at in a fragmentary fashion.[22]

In *The Christian Faith*, Christ is spoken of as the fulfilment of prophecy, in that he is both the climax and the end of the line of prophets whose story is contained in the Old Testament. But how can this fulfilment be of any value when Christian teaching must be based on the New Testament alone? If the Old Testament is simply superfluous for doctrinal purposes, then the tracing of promise and fulfilment from Old to New Testaments is neither legitimate nor necessary as a means of interpreting the work of Christ. The problem is most acute in dealing with the law, for it is the legal spirit against which Schleiermacher reacts most strongly. Two passages in *The Christian Faith* are directly contradictory:

> The priestly office of Christ includes His perfect fulfilment of the law (i.e. His active obedience).[23]

> The active obedience of Christ must not be presented as the perfect fulfilment of the divine law.[24]

Despite Schleiermacher's disclaimers, a major section of his Christology is an exposition of Christ as prophet, priest, and king, in which the Old Testament is used as the context for the interpretation of the significance of Christ.

In the end, the Old Testament remains a problem for Schleiermacher. It illustrates the general problem of what he called scientific dogmatic, which begins with certain general principles, expanding them logically in

---

22. *Saemmtliche Werke*, part I, vol. 8 (*Neue Testament*), 25–26.
23. *Christian Faith*, vol. 2 (104), 451.
24. *Christian Faith*, vol. 2 (104:3), 455.

accordance with the demands of the religious consciousness and the general consciousness of the church, taking into account the confessional statements and the New Testament writings. Neither the religious consciousness nor the literary tradition of Christianity is thoroughly consistent. The Christian interpretation of the Old Testament is a mixture of rejection and acceptance. Schleiermacher exhibited this two-sidedness with regard to it, and in this way shows his fidelity to the tradition of interpretation in the church. But Schleiermacher's tendency to reject the Old Testament is so strong that the counterbalancing tendency is faint, and sometimes invisible. His literary romanticism gave him a love of Greek literature and thought, and with it a contempt for Hebrew writings. This aversion, which seems aesthetic in origin, colored his exegesis and his doctrine and prevented the Old Testament from making any important positive contribution to his theology.

6

The Church as Interpreter

ONE OF THE DISTINCTIVE marks of Schleiermacher's theology is the importance which he gives to the concept of the church. The church is a historical continuum, originating with the gift of the Spirit at Pentecost and continuing as the instrument of Christ's redemptive activity until the present time. For the individual, to be redeemed by Christ and to be in fellowship with the Christian church is one and the same thing. The redemptive activity of Christ is mediated through the God-consciousness of the believing community and is transmitted through the proclamation of the gospel. Proclamation is an essential function of the church, one of the invariable marks which continues through history, irrespective of changed times or local circumstance. The Scriptures themselves are part of this proclamation, an expression of the religious self-consciousness of the early church. In subsequent periods, each living part of the church has had its own distinctive mode of expression, and through this expression, faith has been perpetuated.

Schleiermacher gives a distinctive place to church tradition in the transmission of belief. In his dogmatic system, quotations from Reformation creeds are prefixed to sections of *The Christian Faith* as expressions of received teaching, in the light of which contemporary propositions must be formulated. Consideration of how Schleiermacher uses tradition for the formulation of his dogmatic system, with reference both to the Protestant confessions and to previous dogmatic systems, would form the subject of an independent study. Here, the question is relevant to his treatment of biblical texts: In what way is his interpretation of the Bible determined by traditional interpretation?

Schleiermacher interprets the Bible in the light of what he considers to be the general spirit of Protestant teaching. In some cases, the Evangelical creeds provide limits beyond which interpretation must not stray. In others, the tradition of Protestantism provides a general concept which may be used for interpreting passages and sections of the New Testament. In others, the spirit of Protestantism requires that texts be given quite novel interpretations, because previous theologies had not been sufficiently thoroughgoing in applying their own principles. The question then becomes that of seeing the way in which Schleiermacher uses traditional interpretation as a stimulus and as a restraint within his own theology and exegesis.

The importance of the teaching of the church as a constituent element in theology is first worked out by Schleiermacher in his *Brief Outline on the Study of Theology*. In it, he calls theology a "positive science" whose propositions are formulated and arranged systematically in order to serve the practical function of ordering the essential thought of the church. The purpose of theology is to provide training for leaders of the church, so that they may gain knowledge of the people whom they are leading:

> Good leadership of the church also requires a knowledge of the whole community which is to be led: (a) of its situation at any given time, and (b) of its past, with the realisation that this community, regarded as a whole, is a historical entity, and that its present condition can be adequately grasped only when it is viewed as a product of the past.[1]

Theology is not, therefore, the concern of everyone in the church, but only of those who take part in leadership, leadership having as wide an interpretation and as free a form as possible. Theology includes theoretical knowledge and practical instruction, and aims at a wide account of the range of theological subjects, to provide the broadest possible background of knowledge. The work of the theologian, if it is pursued with integrity, must promote the welfare of the church, and therefore theology is never purely theoretical or disinterested.

Every area of theological study is directed toward understanding the distinctiveness of Christianity. Dogmatic theology is one of a series of historical studies which provide knowledge of the past and present situations of the church. These studies begin with exegesis, and then proceed to the history of Christianity and the present condition of the church. The progress of Christianity may be viewed from several perspectives, but a fairly

---

1. *Saemmtliche Werke*, part I, vol. 1 (*Kurze Darstellung*), 26.

general division within the subject is that between "church history," which deals with the events of the Christian community, and "history of dogma," which develops the religious ideas of the community as they are expressed in doctrine. In a similar way, knowledge of the present church may be divided between the social condition of the church, in its internal constitution and external relations, and the doctrine which is characteristic of the church's present life in any given area. It is this latter discipline to which the name "dogmatic theology" is given:

> The systematic representation of doctrine which is current at any given time, whether for the church in general, when division does not prevail, or for any particular party within the church, we designate by the term "dogmatics" or "dogmatic theology."[2]

THE CHRISTIAN FAITH

In *The Christian Faith*, the definition of dogmatics is only slightly different from that given in the *Brief Outline*: "Dogmatic Theology is the science which systematizes the doctrine prevalent in a Christian Church at a given time."[3] By doctrine, in this definition, Schleiermacher does not mean merely those statements which are stated in the creeds and confessions of the churches. Doctrine is the entire body of teaching material within the church which is presented to, and found acceptable by, the general religious opinion of the people. Propositions of doctrine first arise as the expression of an individual religious self-consciousness, but they become truly dogmatic only when they are accepted publicly. New approaches and improvements in teaching originate in popular religious literature and preaching, and they become part of the official doctrine when they are accepted as expressions of the general consciousness of faith. Thus, the material from which doctrinal statements are drawn is very broad. It includes the entire spectrum of religious self-consciousness and the total expression of religious emotion. From the mass of dogmatic propositions, only those are regarded as significant which are judged to be ecclesiastical; those which are regarded as heretical must be rejected. Thus, there is built up a system of orthodox doctrine which contains those propositions which have commended themselves to the consensus of Christian opinion over a period of time. The necessary consequence of this approach is that dogmatic material is not principally composed of biblical

---

2. *Saemmtliche Werke*, part I, vol. 1 (*Kurze Darstellung*), 97.
3. *Christian Faith*, vol. 1 (19), 88.

statements.[4] The Bible is not a systematic work, and neither the language nor the arrangement of the Bible makes it a suitable source for a scientific dogmatic. Only parts of the New Testament are didactic in form, and none of it is properly systematic in arrangement. Such didactic sections as do exist occur in letters, or other occasional writings, and any attempt to collect them in a systematic form would be more likely to confuse than to form a coherent whole. A scriptural dogmatic, in contrast to a scientific one, would lack proper arrangement and would sacrifice important doctrines to elements which had only a passing relevance in the New Testament itself. The language of the Bible is indefinite and ambiguous, and it is unsuitable for expressing current Christian belief. Because of the varying character of biblical propositions, they are no more suitable as prooftexts than as constitutive statements. The method of proving doctrines by prooftexts, in Schleiermacher's view, is a harmful one, leading to rigidity in doctrine and dishonesty in exegesis. The proper way in which passages of Scripture should be related to doctrine is by showing that the same religious emotion was characteristic of the doctrine and of the verses cited. This can only be done properly by maintaining a wide view of the Bible, a view which relies on large sections and avoids stressing individual passages separated from their contexts.

A contradiction is immediately apparent in this approach.

Schleiermacher's conception of the relationship between dogmatics and the Bible is not what was generally prevalent in the church of his day. It did not conform to the strict standards of orthodoxy in either the Reformed or the Lutheran churches. It certainly did not represent the views of pietistic groups, and yet it was both too pious and too ecclesiastical to be an expression of the Enlightenment. Since Schleiermacher's day, there has never been a theological school, or an ecclesiastical body, which has adopted his formulations as a general theological basis. In his view, individual expressions of faith, the common spirit of the church, and the careful examination of biblical passages should not diverge, but rather converge in a single viewpoint. In this case, as in others, reality does not conform to the ideal, and Schleiermacher, far from expounding the mind of the church, gives expression to a viewpoint which is highly distinctive and individual. The consequences for subsequent theology have been very serious. The failure to unite biblical doctrine, personal self-consciousness, and common belief in a single system has issued in a climate of theology in which each goes its own way. In one corner, there is the theology which regards exposition of the revealed word as the only legitimate dogmatic task; in another, there is the theology of personal existence, whose aim is the establishment of authentic humanity;

---

4. *Christian Faith*, vol. 1 (27), 112. See also (27:3), 115–16, (27:4) 116–17.

and in another, there is sociological theology, which expounds religion as a type of cultural expression. It is this last approach to theology which is said to have arisen from Schleiermacher, but it does not consistently represent his viewpoint. Schleiermacher insists on a unique place for Jesus Christ in faith and theology, and this prevents him from really representing the "history of religions" school of thought.

For Schleiermacher, the Bible is not the source of dogmatic material, but it is the norm for dogmatic statement.[5] All presentations of Christian faith are expressions of the religious self-consciousness of some person who had been stirred by a previous expression of faith. Such presentations are ultimately to be traced to Christ, whose preaching was the expression of his perfect God-consciousness. From his preaching sprang the faith of the apostles. Their preaching was the beginning of the faith of the early church, and also the source of the books of the New Testament. Subsequent preaching has been based on apostolic faith and the Scriptures. The grounds of faith now are the same as the grounds of the faith of the original disciples: the communication of the consciousness of God on the basis of Christ's original and perfect God-consciousness. Of all such communication subsequent to its own time, the New Testament remains the enduring norm. The uniqueness of the New Testament stems from the fact that only in the apostolic age did members of the church have a living, personal intuition of Christ. Because of this relationship, the church was able to discern the proper difference between what was canonical and what was apocryphal in the expression of contemporary religious self-consciousness. Many debasing influences were brought to bear upon the presentation of the Christian message, particularly in the form of Jewish modes of thought and morality, which were not authentic parts of the gospel. The discrepancy between these influences and the lively spirit of Christ's teaching, known to the early Christians from personal memory, caused the church to reject them. Later ages, when faced with a challenge of the same sort, have no such direct remembrance to provide a standard of choice. Instead, subsequent Christians have the New Testament canon as an authority, normative for all teaching of faith. Every part of the New Testament does not deserve equal authority. Some passages are casual expressions, vague in meaning and uncertain in authority. In other passages, it has been necessary for the church to reach a decision, accepting certain teaching as derived from Christ and rejecting other material as not so derived; such passages have a definite authority for subsequent teaching. Among later expressions of Christian faith, it is not necessary for statements to have their origin in biblical sentences, because

---

5. *Christian Faith*, vol. 2 (129), 594. See also (131) 604, (128:2), 592–93.

the Holy Spirit causes original expression of genuine faith to arise in every age. But the Spirit will not prompt any expression which is entirely out of harmony with the original statements of faith. Hence, nothing can be classed as truly Christian which is incompatible with the sense of the New Testament. This position of the New Testament is absolutely unique within Christianity, and no other writing can ever gain equal authority with it as the norm of teaching in the church.

The New Testament is the norm for the church's doctrine, but it is also true to say that doctrine is the norm for interpreting the New Testament.[6] Every proposition in a Protestant dogmatic must first be tested on the basis of the Evangelical confessional documents, as a means of indirect appeal to the Scriptures. These confessions claim the Scriptures as their basis, and any comparison of teaching with them is an indirect comparison with Scripture. But these confessions demonstrate what is distinctive Protestant doctrine, and give interpretations of the Bible which are standard for Protestant teaching. This is particularly true with respect to points of difference with the Roman Catholic Church: Roman Catholic teaching may sanction one particular use of a passage of the New Testament, while Protestant confessions sanction another. Protestant communities are recognized as such by their adherence to these Protestant modes of interpretation. Confessional statements may be further reformed, either because they do not properly adhere to a scriptural basis at certain points, or because they do not sufficiently emphasize the distinctive Evangelical character of some particular doctrine. In general, however, the confessions express the sense of Scripture as received by the church.

The doctrinal tradition upon which Schleiermacher is relying is the tradition of a particular branch of the church as it exists at a particular time and place. Within a dogmatic system, there are elements which represent matter which is common to all, and others which represent the personal viewpoint of the author of the system. The common matter, in the first place, includes those doctrines which are characteristic of the whole church, in all its branches, Eastern and Western, Roman Catholic and Protestant. Next, it deals with those doctrines which express the characteristic spirit of the particular branch of the church to which the system belongs. The emphasis given to universal and particular types of doctrine is a matter of choice for an author, consistent with the relations prevailing among the branches of the church at a particular time. The historical situation of nineteenth-century Germany persuaded Schleiermacher that there could be no rapprochement of Roman Catholic and Protestant churches at that time, and hence it was

---

6. *Christian Faith*, vol. 1 (27:1), 112–14.

necessary to stress the distinctive marks of doctrine, and hence the distinctive ways of interpreting Scripture. Among the Protestant churches, the matter was different, and Schleiermacher considered it necessary to stress points of agreement, and to ignore points of difference between Reformed and Lutheran theologies. Hence, the doctrinal tradition which he sought to develop was the common heritage of German Protestantism.

Within the Evangelical confessions, certain doctrines are sometimes expressed in a polemical manner against other Protestant groups. Such polemical elements are evidence of the character of all symbolic writings as occasional documents, whose composition reflects the circumstances of the church when they were written. Their mode of expression cannot, therefore, be adequate for all time. Some doctrines are expressed in a manner which is merely traditional without being worked out in a distinctively Protestant way. In others, doctrines are rejected precipitately, without sufficient recognition of the true Protestant character of the rejected expression. Hence, the confessions cannot be applied in a literal fashion, but only in accordance with their spirit. As the confessions represent Lutheran and Reformed viewpoints, Schleiermacher regards their spirit as embracing everything which authentically expresses Lutheran or Reformed opinion, and as preventing interpretation of essential doctrines in a way which is agreeable to neither party. In this way, the Protestant tradition sets limits for biblical interpretation by rejecting certain concepts as contrary to the spirit of the two major Protestant groups. Both tendencies in Evangelical doctrine affirm justification by faith alone, and this *sola fide* is a constituent principle in any Protestant system. It is a key for the interpretation of Scripture, and in some cases is to be used beyond the practice of the Reformers themselves.

For Schleiermacher, in some areas, the Protestant churches had simply continued previous practices, and the ongoing work of the Spirit required that doctrine be further developed beyond the bounds of traditional Protestant interpretation. In some cases, the spirit of Protestantism must be carried further to revise and correct the tradition, but in others, the religious self-consciousness of the present must interpret the Bible afresh and affirm meanings which the Reformers overlooked or rejected. Examples of these various treatments accorded to the tradition of the church are to be found both in *The Christian Faith* and in Schleiermacher's sermons.

PROTESTANT TRADITION RESPECTING THE LORD'S SUPPER

Schleiermacher's discussion of communion in *The Christian Faith* is an example of his use of Protestant confessions as limiting concepts.[7] Protestant interpretations of the significance of the Lord's Supper have varied considerably, and proponents of the various views have quarreled bitterly, but none of the views has freed itself from inconsistency, and none has established itself universally. However, Protestants can regard as acceptable any view which remains within the area between Roman Catholic transubstantiation and Sacramentarian spiritualism. The words included in all the New Testament records of the institution of the Lord's Supper (Mark 14:22 and parallels)—τοῦτό ἐστιν τὸ σῶμά μου ("While they were eating, he took a loaf of bread, and after blessing it he broke it, gave it to them, and said, 'Take; this is my body'" [NRSV])—as interpreted in the Roman Catholic Church, mean not only that Christ is corporeally received by those who partake of communion, but also that the change of substance persists apart from the act of reception. Had it not been for this, Schleiermacher believes that the early Lutherans would not have objected to Roman Catholic eucharistic doctrine. This interpretation allows adoration of the elements, and a conception of magical spiritual impact attached to the elements, altogether apart from participation in the sacrament. Protestant doctrine has consistently denied the presence of Christ apart from the eucharistic action. The purpose of communion, in the Protestant understanding of the sacrament, is to participate in the gift of Christ. Roman Catholic doctrine, advancing beyond common participation to purposes which are quite different, is uniformly rejected. This forms the one limit which is unacceptable to received Protestant teaching.

The other limit is marked by those radical Protestant groups who deny that the gift of Christ is in any way connected with receiving the elements of communion. This point of view, dubbed by Lutheran polemics as Sacramentarianism, emphasizes mere spiritual participation in Christ, of a kind that may be found altogether apart from the communion rite. At best, the reception of Christ and partaking of the elements are connected fortuitously. Such a view destroys any concept of sacramental action and is a misconception of Christ's institution.

Between these two limits, Schleiermacher believes that Protestants are free to affirm any one of several doctrines concerning the presence of Christ. The Evangelical church will accept any view which avoids the danger, on the

---

7. *Christian Faith*, vol. 2 (139–42), 638–57.

one hand, of a magical value in the sacrament, and on the other hand, of the sacrament reduced to a bare sign. There are difficulties in any view which may be adopted. The first problem is caused by the text: none of the narratives of the Last Supper agree fully with any of the others. As a result, we have a continuing uncertainty with respect to the exact words of Christ, and interpretation can be no more certain than the text. By a literal explanation of the words, Lutheran interpretation seeks to maintain the connection between the physical acts and the spiritual benefits derived from them. However, a literal interpretation cannot be made, simultaneously, of all of the words recorded for the giving of the cup. The Zwinglian view is that Christ's command unites spiritual participation in the flesh and blood of Christ with the partaking of the bread and wine. Thus, it recognizes only two things, bodily participation and spiritual effect joined together by the word. But this leaves unexplained why Christ spoke as he did. The Calvinist view is that, along with bodily participation and spiritual effect, we must recognize a real presence of Christ's body and blood present here as nowhere else. This explanation, while avoiding the difficulties of extreme presentations of the Lutheran or Zwinglian types, still lacks a distinct explanation of the relation of body and blood, and in the end, it is no more satisfactory than either of the other two. Schleiermacher hopes that someday an explanation will be worked out which will avoid all of the problems associated with the three distinctive positions, but which will meanwhile affirm that any one of them is acceptable within Protestantism and that all must be recognized as only partially effective.

Schleiermacher makes only a few statements to indicate positively his own position within the limits which he recognizes for Protestant doctrine.[8] In the first place, the institution of the Lord's Supper was a historic event, in which Christ ate with his disciples, and they acted correctly in perpetuating it. Secondly, in accordance with the institution of Christ, his body and blood are administered to those who partake of communion. Thirdly, Christ is spiritually present in the communion. Fourthly, a spiritual benefit is conferred upon those who partake: in particular, the forgiveness of sins, which has its proper locus in the sacrament. Fifthly, the sacrament does not depend on the officiating minister but "every effect flows directly . . . from the Word of institution in which the redeeming . . . love of Christ is not only represented but made newly active."[9] Sixthly, the sacrament is rightly administered when the attempt is made to represent the original action materially and formally, and thus, as far as it is possible, represent it in

---

8. *Christian Faith*, vol. 2 (139), 638, (139:1) 638–39, (139:2) 642–43, (141:1) 651–53.
9. *Christian Faith*, vol. 2 (139), 641.

its essential features. The action involves prayer and sermon, followed by distribution to all partakers of both bread and wine. The whole service is a communal act, the culmination of the public worship of the church.

Schleiermacher assigns a very high value and importance to communion, it being one of the essential and invariable features of the church. In accordance with the general arrangement of *The Christian Faith*, Schleiermacher begins his discussion of the Lord's Supper with an examination of the Christian consciousness. The communion meets a need, which all feel, for strengthened fellowship with Christ and with other Christians. But neither the material action nor the verbal form owes anything in its origin to aspects of the self-consciousness. Both are traced back "by an unbroken tradition to the beginnings of the church, and to the Supper itself as Christ held it with his disciples."[10] The presentation of Christ in the communion always arises out of Scripture. Thus, while Schleiermacher's discussion of the communion is not satisfying at all points, it is not the arbitrarily wishful thinking, which is sometimes represented. It is an interpretation of the relevant passages of Scripture in the light of the developed thought of Protestant theology, within the limits of Lutheran and Reformed tradition.

THE TRUE SPIRIT OF THE REFORMATION

The second way in which the tradition of the church provides a norm for the interpretation of Scripture is by providing a number of key concepts, drawn from Scripture itself, which are used for the description and regulation of all Christian experience. For Schleiermacher, the key concept of the Reformation is justification by faith. In 1830, he preached a series of sermons to celebrate the three-hundredth anniversary of the presentation of the Augsburg Confession.[11][12] In the sermon, on the day of the anniversary itself, he outlines the two major points which are to be derived from the Confession: the outspoken declaration against perverted practices in worship and doctrine, and the central principle of justification in faith:

> The second decisive point is this, that this document, with unbroken clarity, with great earnestness, humility and sincerity of heart grasped and presented the unique key concept of belief that peace with God does not come . . . from our own service; righteousness before God is received when we accept him whom God has sent, in faith from our hearts . . . . This is the key point

10. *Christian Faith*, vol. 2 (139), 639.
11. *Saemmtliche Werke*, part II, vol. 2 (*Vierte-Siebente Sammlung*), 613.
12. See also ch. 5, "Creation."

on which all genuine Protestant Christians always agree. If we abandon this ... then all previous outward agreement becomes worthless. The true spirit of this confession is to hold fast to faith in the Redeemer in whom we see the glory of the only-begotten Son of the Father ... and to lay aside everything else on which a man may set a value.[13]

In a sermon on Galatians 2:16–18[14] which follows in the series, Schleiermacher works out the conception of justification by faith as freedom from law, and uses the idea of freedom as the denial of orthodoxy. In New Testament times, freedom from the law meant that Christians did not have to follow the provisions of the Jewish law. In Reformation times, the concept was interpreted to mean that faith could free men from obedience to a variety of ritual obligations which were not part of the gospel and which were irrelevant to faith. Within German Protestantism of his own day, Schleiermacher believed that the concept of freedom from law meant freedom from a legalistic purity of doctrine. The essential point in his argument is that faith and doctrine are two different things and must be carefully distinguished:

> It is established among us that faith is simply nothing else than the repeatedly renewed movement of the heart which accepts the fellowship offered to us by Christ. Whoever has this must also have a consciousness of it which authenticates this fellowship for him. But a person who barely knows enough about it to stammer ... can live as firmly in this fellowship as one who can please us and stimulate us with the finest and correctest speech on the subject; only in doctrine is the latter better equipped than the former. ... Can firmness of faith ... depend upon how far one immerses oneself in doctrinal thought? ... If not, then faith and doctrine are entirely different things.[15]

Schleiermacher's argument here is similar to that in *The Christian Faith*, where he rejects the connection between faith and knowledge. An increase in knowledge does not necessarily result in an increase in piety; similarly, an increase in the understanding of doctrine cannot be said to entail an increase in faith. He uses the argument drawn from Reformation principles against the practice of the reformers and the Augsburg Confession itself. The Confession had confused the concepts of faith and doctrine, and subsequent controversy had altered the concept of faith until it became the idea of correct belief. The consequence was the erection of a literal

---

13. *Saemmtliche Werke*, part II, vol. 2 (*Vierte-Siebente Sammlung*), 629–30.
14. *Saemmtliche Werke*, part II, vol. 2 (*Vierte-Siebente Sammlung*), 637.
15. *Saemmtliche Werke*, part II, vol. 2 (*Vierte-Siebente Sammlung*), 649.

standard which was legally binding and which was used to compel faith. This, for Schleiermacher, is a perversion of the best effects of the Reformation, and is nothing more than the reinstatement of righteousness by works. Its effect is to force the majority of Christians to blindly accept whatever is written by the teachers who are established in the tradition of the church. To be true to the Reformation and to the Augsburg Confession itself, it is necessary to be free from adherence to the letter of doctrine, and in its place put obedience to the living spirit. Instead of doctrine, faith is to be equated with a disposition resulting from free impulse in the heart.

What is true of the interpretation of the doctrine of the church is also true of the interpretation of the Bible. An attention to the letter of Scripture which is overly scrupulous will result in a denial of the Spirit which speaks through the Bible. Absolute literalism makes of the Bible a dead letter, and obedience to it can never bring our hearts to the love of God. The text of the Bible includes many incidents and sayings which are recounted according to the manner of the times, and we must interpret not according to the manner of the times, but according to the Spirit which is seen in God's love in Christ. The chief use which Schleiermacher makes of this distinction between letter and spirit is in connection with the Old Testament. We have seen his general rejection of the Old Testament writings and his specific rejection of Mosaic law as sources for Christian teaching. The character of the Old Testament is designated as law, whereas the New Testament is the witness to the Spirit. Schleiermacher's interpretation of *sola fide* is a factor relevant to his treatment of the Old Testament. Any reliance upon the Old Testament implies a concept of righteousness based on works, works being interpreted as including written records, laws, and facts of history. The New Testament alone is the necessary and sufficient norm of faith which is based on Christ alone. Thus, a Reformation principle is used, in a way unimagined by the Reformers themselves, to provide means of interpreting and judging large sections of the Bible, and also books, passages, and verses of the New Testament.

CORRECTING THE TRADITION

Schleiermacher believed the Christian tradition to be in the process of constant development. The form of Christian life changes in accordance with the principles of general historical progress, and religious ideas advance in various historical stages appropriate to the stage of general religious life. For Schleiermacher, Christianity itself is an absolutely new beginning in religion; the Reformation was not a completely new start, but only the beginning of a new development within Christianity. Now the church must progress to a more developed stage of life, and express its teaching in terms appropriate to the higher stage. Thus, the Protestant tradition must develop new forms and new statements of doctrine. Some of the development comes by way of extending the principles already set forth at an earlier stage. Some development comes through the critical examination of ideas of ancient lineage which have been accepted by habit within the Christian community and reaffirmed with too much ease. A third mode of development is more radical than the others; it comes when the current expression of the religious self-consciousness requires the abandonment of concepts of religion which have adequately served an older and more primitive community, but which are no longer serviceable. Each of these developments in theological conceptions must have its counterpart in modes of biblical interpretation.

Schleiermacher's treatment of law and gospel is one example in which the spirit of the Reformation is used to correct doctrinal statements and approaches to biblical interpretation widely current within the Protestant tradition. We have already seen how this concept of law is used to reject the whole Protestant tradition of prescriptive ethics, and in particular the specific Lutheran formulations on the threefold use of the divine law.[16]

With respect to some other doctrines, Schleiermacher believes that the Reformers had simply taken them over from the old tradition of the church without giving them new treatment or sufficient scrutiny. In these matters, the work of the Reformation is still to be done, and it would result in conclusions different from those accepted in the Protestant creeds. An outstanding example of this is Schleiermacher's treatment of the Trinity.[17] In *The Christian Faith*, the doctrine of the Trinity is virtually relegated to an appendix, not because it is false, but because it is a secondary doctrine, derived from other doctrines, and because in its formulation there are a number of unsettled questions which call for thorough reexamination.

In still other cases, doctrines affirmed in the confessions with a basis of strong biblical support have to be revised or discarded because they do not adequately express the spirit of love which is the mind of Christ. One such doctrine is that of the wrath of God. As has been noted above, Schleiermacher regarded the wrath of God as a concept applicable only to the time of preparation under the law and not as part of Christian proclamation to those who have responded in faith to Christ.[18] In one of the sermons in

---

16. See ch. 5, "Ethics."
17. *Christian Faith*, vol. 2 (170–72), 738–47.
18. See ch. 3, "Interpreting Pauline Doctrine." See also *Saemmtliche Werke*, part II, vol. 2 (*Vierte-Siebente Sammlung*), 725.

the series on the Augsburg Confession, he denies the whole conception of the wrath of God in connection with Christian theology, despite the teaching of the confession. There is no need to retain such a conception, and to the extent that we do retain it, we separate ourselves from the true spirit of Christianity. Schleiermacher maintains that the support for the doctrine in the teaching of Christ is very slight, and that such instances as do occur are to be explained as modes of speech which Christ used to make his message vivid without thereby expressing any idea which was essential to the gospel. In the sermon, Schleiermacher discusses the parable of the king's marriage feast from Matthew 22. He claims that the condemnation which the king pronounces against the man who came without a proper garment has no proper analogy in the acts of God:

> If we wish to apply to God what he [the Lord] says about the anger of the king in a literal manner, we must in the same way apply to him all the rest that appears here, namely, that the king sent out his army and destroyed many cities. Certainly it cannot be denied that in the writings of the apostles there is talk of the wrath of God in a number of places, even in the writings of Paul who ... presents Christianity to us as the office of reconciliation. But let us not forget what is relevant here: the apostle is speaking to those who either belonged directly to the people of the old covenant, or, if their connection was more distant, were brought to a knowledge of Christianity through the people of the old covenant. We know that in the old covenant a great deal is said about the wrath of God; the law and the prophets, are full of representations of this anger, and wrath, and warnings which spring from it. But it is in this connection that the apostle says. . . . Whoever is in Christ is a new creature; what is old is past, all has become new. To the old which is past, for all who in Christ are become a new creature, belongs above all any such representation of the wrath of God. Considering it carefully it is most consistent to regard this as belonging to the means which God found necessary to use in the then existing condition of the world and of the human race....
>
> In general ... let us all conclude that this representation of the wrath of God can find no room whatever in the fruitful knowledge which a Christian may have of God.[19]

Thus, the wrath of God is seen as a concept from a more primitive stage in the history of religion, but one which must be discarded in an age when ideas are more developed and more mature.

19. *Saemmtliche Werke*, part II, vol. 2 (*Vierte-Siebente Sammlung*), 727–29.

For Schleiermacher, the conception of the wrath of God can have no place in Christian consciousness. It is an idea which belonged to the old covenant, which is abrogated in Christ. In Christ, the principle is love, and any concept of fear toward God is a denial of that love and of the Christian spirit. The sermon is similar to his discussion of the justice of God in *The Christian Faith*.[20] There it is denied that God's justice can be considered retributive in any sense. Retribution implies that the injured party can derive enjoyment from the harming of the one who has inflicted the injury. To think of God as acting in this way is to project a very primitive religious consciousness, one which conceives of God as susceptible to irritation. For Schleiermacher, this has no place in any developed Christian conception of God. Any proper understanding of divine justice must be based on the fact that the real purpose of punishment is to deter, and that punishment can have a place in religious conceptions only when the God-consciousness is so weak that some other means is necessary to prevent such a development of the lower aspects of human nature that they dominate the self-consciousness. Thus, the entire concept of God's anger is dismissed because it does not conform to the best religious ideals of the age.

Similarly, we must reject all propositions within the body of received Christian teaching which condemn those who believe differently from ourselves. In another sermon in the same series, Schleiermacher rejects those sections of the Augsburg Confession which denounced differing opinions.[21] Many of these condemnations were based on inadequate grounds and were formulated in the heat of controversy. Even where they were correctly directed against dangerous tendencies in the church, they ought not to have been expressed. The ethical principle which should guide us when we are dealing with those who do not share our ideas is based on Christ's saying (Luke 6:37): "Do not judge, and you will not be judged; do not condemn, and you will not be condemned. Forgive, and you will be forgiven" (NRSV). There is no assurance that majorities in ecclesiastical assemblies are closer to the truth than minorities, and to break fellowship with other Christians because they differ from us is merely to destroy the fellowship in which we all need to share as Christians. In this sense, those who condemn others effectively condemn themselves. What applies to contemporary doctrinal controversy, and to our consideration of Reformation doctrine, also applies when interpreting texts of the Bible. Anathemas have no place in our judgment as Christians. The characteristic ideas of the New Testament are positive and constructive in promoting fellowship with God, and are expressed

---

20. *Christian Faith*, vol. 1 (84), 345.
21. *Saemmtliche Werke*, part II, vol. 2 (*Vierte-Siebente Sammlung*), 710.

in such words as "love," "faith," "reconciliation," and "forgiveness." Rejection on account of doctrine, and broken fellowship because of disagreement within the New Testament (as elsewhere), are not expressive of the true spirit of the gospel.

Behind this whole discussion is Schleiermacher's conception of doctrine as the expression of religious self-consciousness: all doctrine is opinion, including elements of truth and error. The New Testament is also the expression of the religious self-consciousness of certain members of the early church. It too is not free from error, but it is the irreplaceable standard of doctrine because it expounds the God-consciousness of those who were nearest to Christ. Doctrinal formulations of later periods do not share this characteristic of immediateness, and so they have a secondary character. But within the development of doctrine, ideas are purified as the church progresses, and formulations of later periods are superior to earlier products because they represent a greater awareness of the consequences to which earlier propositions may lead. Biblical interpretation develops along with the development of doctrine, increasing in definiteness and taking new forms in accordance with the development of language. In this process, some biblical concepts are rejected as outmoded, others are restated in terms better understood in a new age, and others are given places of importance which previously they did not have because the religious self-consciousness of an earlier age did not recognize their true value.

It has been said that in Schleiermacher's development of the constitutive role which tradition plays in theology, he overcame a blind spot in Protestant theology.[22] For Schleiermacher, tradition does not constitute a deposit of truth; instead, it consists of ongoing proclamation. The New Testament is the record of the original proclamation, and, as normative proclamation, it is the starting point of all subsequent preaching. As such, the New Testament is part of the tradition, the constitutive and normative basis of the tradition. The key concept in his idea of the church is that of proclamation, which is the means by which the church transmits the total effective influence of Christ from age to age, and at the same time, the direct expression of the religious self-consciousness of the church at any one time. Proclamation depends upon the Scriptures; no course of preaching and no system of doctrine can commend itself unless it conforms to the standard of the New Testament. On the other hand, proclamation interprets Scripture by giving expression to biblical ideas as they have commended themselves to the church and have found a place in the self-consciousness of the preacher. As such, Scripture and tradition do not stand against one

---

22. Wilburn, "Role of Tradition in Schleiermacher's Theology," 306.

another as competing authorities. They are contained together within the proclamation of the church, so that the Bible determines the content of the tradition, and the tradition interprets the content of the Bible.

7

Some Remarks about Schleiermacher's Exegesis

SCHLEIERMACHER'S EXEGESIS IS TOO big a topic to be properly handled in this study. As has been remarked previously, a thorough study of the subject must await the publication of his exegetical manuscripts. Without them, we have no knowledge of Schleiermacher's evaluation of the Greek text or of the way in which he dealt with the vocabulary and structure of various passages. The most detailed studies which are available, his articles on 1 Timothy and Colossians 1:15–20, show that he was capable of subjecting passages to very close examination. This lies almost entirely below the surface in his preaching and dogmatic writing. Even in his expository preaching there is almost no indication of his opinion about textual and structural details. A study could be made of his expository preaching to find the passages which are stressed and those which are not, but the material for such a study would be very extensive, and there is no literature available which would provide any guide for approaching it.

In the present study, we offer merely some comments on Schleiermacher's exegesis, based on an examination of the article on Colossians, and of the references which Schleiermacher makes to Romans 8 in *The Christian Faith* and the four volumes of his general preaching. The contrast between the types of exegesis offered in the two is very apparent. The article is a detailed examination of the Greek, paying careful attention to structure and vocabulary. The references in *The Christian Faith* are bare allusions to the text, often with no hint that any careful study of the passage has been made. This contrast is deceptive. One would not know from reading *The Christian Faith* that Schleiermacher had given any special attention to the passage from Colossians, but one may conjecture that his article includes work which was done before the writing of the dogmatic. After consideration of Colossians and Romans, a few general remarks will be made about the way Schleiermacher uses texts in his sermons.

Two points may be made about his exegesis, in confidence that they would be sustained in any detailed inquiry into this exegesis. First, Schleiermacher seeks to set out the general meaning of the New Testament, of an author, or of a work. He is therefore concerned with gaining an impression of the whole, and, in the light of that impression, to interpret any individual passage, sentence, or phrase. No particular passage can be allowed to contradict the general impression, and where this seems to occur, the particular verses must be explained away or else rejected as part of the original text. The context is more important than any particular text. Secondly, Schleiermacher is concerned with the structure of language. Therefore, he gives a great deal of attention to linguistic considerations, stressing grammatical construction and the use of words. Schleiermacher does not give much attention to variations in the text on the basis of varying manuscripts of the New Testament, but he does regard it as legitimate to base important conclusions on logical and grammatical relationships among words and phrases.

As a consequence of the first of these tendencies, Schleiermacher is more readily found examining a text so as to demolish it, rather than to use it constructively. According to his principles, positive doctrine must be drawn from a general impression and not from an individual passage. Thus, the passages which are most important for his theological construction are assumed or merely alluded to. It has been noted above that Schleiermacher regarded his whole dogmatic theology as a commentary on John 1:14, and within *The Christian Faith* there are at least two occasions when his understanding of that verse and of 2 Corinthians 5:17–19 is the center of his argument, although he makes no specific citation.[1] The only exegesis which can really establish a doctrine is the exegesis of the whole of the New Testament, or at least the exegesis of the work of an author or of an entire New Testament book. The detailed study of a particular passage may aid in this general interpretation, but it cannot establish it. Such study, however, can be used to prevent the use of a passage for a contrary purpose. Exegesis of a few verses is thus a more ready weapon in a negative cause than in a positive one.

---

1. *Christian Faith*, vol. 2 (96:3), 396–98, (99), 421–24.

The instances when Schleiermacher uses a scriptural argument to reach a conclusion at variance with received doctrine are more apparent than those in which he uses such an argument to establish a main point of his theology. In his view, this would not mean that his thought is any the less scriptural in its basis than a system bolstered with prooftexts. For Schleiermacher, prooftexts are verses torn from their context and thus falsely interpreted. The only true exegesis is that founded upon context which yields a general impression.

What is the source of Schleiermacher's general impression? This is a question to which an answer cannot be finally given. It is the chief problem of Schleiermacher's theology and of his biblical interpretation. It is unlikely that his exegetical manuscripts would solve the problem any more than any other particular part of his writing. In part, the impression is gained from the New Testament. It will be seen, in the discussion of the article on Colossians, that Schleiermacher concerns himself with the writings of the Greek fathers, together with modern interpreters, to help him gain that impression of the teaching of the New Testament. In part, Schleiermacher's impression is drawn from his own general philosophy. His concept of knowledge and his principles of literary interpretation condition the way he reads Colossians and Romans and other parts of the Bible.

"ON COLOSSIANS 1:15–20"

In his article "On Colossians 1:15–20," Schleiermacher acknowledges that it is a passage which is very important for the consideration of the nature and work of Christ.[2] However, he maintains that his approach is purely hermeneutical, without any prior dogmatic interests or presuppositions. Because this passage has no proper parallel in other places in the New Testament, its form is of great significance. Grammatical structure is the starting point and the main factor in his exegesis. In Schleiermacher's opinion, there are only two sentences from verse 3 to verse 23, one ending at verse 8, and the other at the end of verse 23. The only other possible sentence ending is in verse 16, after *powers*, but Schleiermacher rules this out. The two main verbs of the section are *we give thanks* in verse 3, and *we have not ceased praying* in verse 9. All the clauses from verses 9 to 23 are subordinate, depending on the verb in verse 9. Within these clauses, the subject changes, at first being the addressees of the letter, in verse 15 becoming *God*, and in verse 15 changing to the *Son*. Verse 13 speaks of deliverance and our transfer to the kingdom of the Son, and this theme is taken up again in verses 21–23. Verses 15–20

2. *Saemmtliche Werke*, part I, vol. 2 (*Kolosser*), 361–92.

are to be seen not as a digression from the theme, but as an amplification of the basis for our reconciliation. They are thus to be linked with the verses which immediately precede and follow them.

Verses 15–20 consist of two correlative groups of clauses. Schleiermacher's division is placed at a different point from that chosen by most interpreters: he divides the passage in the middle of verse 18. Thus, the two sections both begin with the pronoun *he*, referring back to verse 13, and the two groups of clauses are descriptions of Jesus Christ. The parallelism between the sections is very striking. Verses 15 and 16 correspond to verses 18 and 19. Both begin by a descriptive clause completed by an explanation introduced by *for*. The clause at the end of verse 18, introduced by *that*, is to be understood parenthetically so that the similarity of the two structures may be preserved. One proceeds, *he is the image . . . for in him all things were created*; the other, *he is the beginning . . . that in him all the fullness of God was pleased to dwell.* Verse 20 is seen as the completion of verses 18 and 19, just as verses 16–18 are the completion of verses 15 and 16. These verses are also parallel in structure, each being built around two verbs, *were created* and *held together* in the one case, *reconcile* and *make peace* in the other. The wording of the end of verse 16, *all things were created through him and for him*, is very similar to that at the beginning of verse 20, *and through him to reconcile to himself all things,* although the grammatical relationships are different. In each of the two main sections, the introductory pronoun has a phrase in apposition to it which gives further witness to the general parallel structure: *first-born of all creation* (v. 15) and *first-born from the dead* (v. 18). The general parallel structure of the two main sections is the chief literary feature of verses 15–20, and provides the basic framework on the basis of which interpretation may proceed.

The relationship of the two sections to one another is the matter which Schleiermacher considers next:

> If we consider the two main sections we may roughly outline their content as follows: Christ is the image of God because everything was made in him, and Christ is first from the dead because the entire fullness wishes to dwell in him. It may be said that the exposition of the first one takes us right out of the moral sphere, which we consider as the realm of the Son, into the sphere of nature. In contrast, the second confines us in the moral sphere, since *and you* of v. 21 is a direct consequence of *all things* of v. 20, which is very closely connected with *all the fullness*.[3]

---

3. *Saemmtliche Werke*, part I, vol. 2 (*Kolosser*), 330 (emphasis original).

Schleiermacher advances this explanation in order to refute it. Its consequence, he says, would be that the Christ through whom everything was made would be the divine nature alone, or in the phrases of traditional theology, the Second Person of the Trinity. The Christ who was firstborn from the dead would specifically exclude this divine person as one who could have no part in death. Such an approach would mean that, strictly speaking, the subject of the first clause and that of the second are different. The grammar makes this impossible, as does the parallel development of the two groups of clauses:

> When Christ called himself Son of God, or called God his Father, he was not distinguishing one nature from another the whole expressive person (*den redenden ganz*), the whole Jesus of Nazareth who at the same time was the Christ. There are no passages in the New Testament in which this expression means the one nature or the other in Christ; it is always the whole undivided Christ. If Paul had intended, in referring back to *son*, in one place to speak only of the one, in the other place of the other nature in Christ, he would have needed to supply a further qualification in each case, by which the implied contrast between the two was made clear.[4]

Schleiermacher concludes from this that we have no right to refer Christ, the Second Person of the Trinity prior to the incarnation, because Paul can only have had the whole undivided Christ in mind. The concern for the unity of the personality of Christ, so evident here, is an example of Schleiermacher's hermeneutical approach, which we have seen in other sections. Jesus Christ, in order to truly have communicated with us, must exhibit a life-unity which we may understand. His true individuality depends on this life-unity, and therefore, in Schleiermacher's view, to speak of his action as being the function of one nature or another within the one person is both artificial and misleading.

As a result, Schleiermacher denies the common exegesis of this passage, which ascribes to Christ a direct part in the original creation. He asserts that the word κτίζειν does not properly refer to the act of creation. The places in the Septuagint where κτίζειν is used, whether it translates ברה [BARAH] or other Hebrew words, are not references to an original creation out of nothing, but to the founding and establishing of things in the course of the development of the world. He maintains that the same is true also of all the places where Paul uses the word κτίζειν (1 Cor 11:19; 1 Tim 4:3; Col 3:10).

---

4. *Saemmtliche Werke*, part I, vol. 2 (*Kolosser*), 331 (italics mine).

In the phrase *firstborn of all creation*, Schleiermacher refers the word *creation* to the establishing and ordering of human affairs. The firstborn is the first member of the human order, on which all others are dependent. He explains *image of the invisible God* as meaning that Christ makes the Father visible. In Romans 11:36, it is God from whom, through whom, and to whom all things exist. Christ's function as the image of God is to show God forth in that everything exists in him. The entire clause after *for in him* refers back to the function of Christ in showing forth the creator. This work is the work of the whole Christ, and by it, things are given a new nature in accordance with the image of God. Schleiermacher refers to Colossians 3:10 in this connection. Thus, Christ's relationship to the work of creation is that through him everything achieves its final form.

Schleiermacher considers that the history of the interpretation of this passage displays all kinds of wild speculation. Throughout his discussion, he makes references to certain of the Greek fathers, and as examples of speculation he mentions the variety of explanations of the words *thrones, dominions, principalities,* and *powers*. There is no need to refer these to orders of existence beyond human nature, when they can perfectly easily refer to ordinary concepts of society. Except for *dominions*, all of the words can be considered as referring to offices or titles belonging to government officers, other public officials, or even teachers. The one word which is unique to the New Testament, *dominions*, should be explained on the basis of its context, and with *thrones* might be interpreted as a term relating to government or else to the position of an instructor. There is no need for an otherworldly interpretation. This also applies to the contrast of heaven and earth, of the visible and the invisible in verse 16. Schleiermacher spiritualizes the concept of heaven so that the phrase *things in heaven*[5] means that which is related to Christ. In a similar way, *things on earth* is to be explained as that which belongs to the civil order, and anything which comes under the regulation of law. Christ is thus linked to what is heavenly, but in addition, everything which has a direct or indirect influence upon what is heavenly is to be seen as established in him and as attaining its perfection in him. Thus, in a sense, all existence can be related to him. This is the meaning of the statement that Christ is the head of the church. All things in the spiritual realm are established and held together by him, and the human community in which the Spirit operates is the church, which in all things is dependent upon him. The first section (vv. 15–18a) is summed up by saying that Christ is the image of God in all aspects of human life, and that Christ is related to the

---

5. *Saemmtliche Werke*, part I, vol. 2 (*Kolosser*), 340. Schleiermacher includes the word in this phrase and the succeeding one. He makes no comment about its place in the text.

world of men in the same way in which God himself is related to the world as a whole. His place as head of the church signifies his headship of the fellowship through which everything gains its true worth, and in which the human spirit is perfected.

This first section may be related to the second (vv. 18b–20) by saying that in one, Christ is the *image of the first-born God* because God has created everything in relation to him, and in the other, Christ is *the beginning, first-born from the dead* because God has willed that the *fullness* should dwell in him.

Schleiermacher regards God as the subject of *was pleased*. For him, this preserves the parallel structure, because he regards God as the subject of the clause in verse 16. The general form of the clause is *God was pleased to have his fullness dwell in him . . . and to make peace and reconcile*. Hence, God is the subject of the verbs subsequent to *was pleased*. For the explanation of *fullness*, Schleiermacher refers back to Romans 11:12, 25, which he regards as the closest comparable passage. There the reference is to the Jews being held back from salvation until the "fullness" of the gentiles is included in the kingdom. Schleiermacher thinks that the passage in Colossians means that there is a "fullness" of both gentiles and Jews, so that the two groups are united in the kingdom under the rule of the Son. This union takes place in the church, and hence it is to the church that *fullness* refers. The work of redemption is God's work through Christ. Part of it is to make peace among the orders of humanity separated from God.[6] The phrases *on earth* and *in heaven* are allusions to this. Our separation from God involves many aspects, including the order of civil society and our religious worship, and these aspects may be taken as characteristic of Greeks and Hebrews.

Making peace among things, whether on earth or in heaven, may thus again refer to the reconciliation of gentiles and Jews in Christ's kingdom, or to the reconciling of man's physical and spiritual nature to God.

In explaining the work by which God makes peace in the cross of Christ, Schleiermacher refers back to what is for him the center of Pauline theology, the abolition of law through the giving of faith in Christ: "Christ has become our peace through the abrogation of the old law, and God has given this peace, in that he sent Christ."[7] He makes reference to Romans 7:1, and to Galatians 2:19, and 3:13, 14, 22, and he notes the connection between Paul's theology and his personal history. In the death of Christ, the law is

---

6. In referring to verse 20, Schleiermacher mentions that some manuscripts omit the second *through him* ("Die latinisirenden Autoritaeten, welche die Worte auslassen"). He draws no conclusions from the remark. See *Saemmtliche Werke*, part I, vol. 2 (*Kolosser*), 352.

7. *Saemmtliche Werke*, part I, vol. 2 (*Kolosser*), 351.

abolished, and after his resurrection, he commands his disciples to make disciples among the gentiles in freedom from the law. Through the cross, Christ has made peace; as the firstborn from the dead, he has made the various parts of divided humanity into genuine members of the kingdom of heaven in a new relationship with God.

At a number of places in his exegesis, Schleiermacher refers to the opinions of Chrysostom and Theodoret. He says that, in general, the opinions of the Greek fathers are valuable for exegesis, because of their knowledge of the language and circumstances of the New Testament. However, he says that because of their habit of fragmenting the text, they are chiefly relevant for matters of detail, and have less authority on questions which concern the overall sense of a passage. Thus, he rejects Chrysostom's opinion that this passage establishes Christ as first above, first in the church, and first in the resurrection. This cannot be a proper interpretation of the passage, because it consists of two sections and not three, as would be required by a threefold conclusion.

Schleiermacher notes Chrysostom's suggestion that all humankind is included in the church in this passage, but he rejects Chrysostom's analogy between the term *first born* and that of foundation stone with respect to Christ. Theodoret sought to make a distinction between πρωτότοκος and πρωτόκJ4FJος as designations of Christ, but Schleiermacher maintains that the one term has all the difficulties of the other. He regards such distinctions as the unfortunate products of polemical theology. Theodoret was the ancient authority for referring fullness to the church, although Schleiermacher regards his reasons for doing so to be inadequate.

Schleiermacher's interpretation of Colossians 1:15–20 must be regarded as eccentric in a number of ways. In particular, his concept of the structure of the passage is given a significance which it does not warrant. By his own admission, the section is a long series of subordinate clauses whose connections are difficult to determine. A high regard for Paul's ability to write complicated sentences whose form is important to their meaning is not a sufficient basis for allowing grammatical conjecture to establish a major theological conclusion. The influence of Schleiermacher's own literary concepts, and his rejection of metaphysical speculation, is very apparent in his exegesis. It provides an excellent example of how he failed to carry out his own intention of proceeding purely hermeneutically, without any presupposed dogmatic purpose. There are philosophical as well as linguistic grounds for his confining of Christ's creative activity to the world of men and for his understanding of *fullness* as a reference to the church.

SCHLEIERMACHER'S REFERENCES TO ROMANS 8

Schleiermacher's handling of the New Testament in his article on Colossians 1 seems very different from what we find in *The Christian Faith* and in the sermons. In the latter two, he does not deal with connected passages, but usually with isolated verses, sometimes quoted to support some point of doctrine, sometimes used incidentally in connection with an argument which rests on grounds not connected with the text. There is no examination of the grammar of a passage, or of its general structure. The eighth chapter of Romans may be taken as an example. It is one of the chapters most frequently cited in *The Christian Faith*, and one which is mentioned frequently in sermons. In the following pages, all of the references to this chapter in *The Christian Faith* and in the first four volumes of sermons will be considered. Schleiermacher does not give a sustained exposition of Romans in any of his works, and it will be seen that he does not deal at any time with chapter 8 as a whole. His references do not set the verses in their place as part of the chapter, but it is still true to say that context is more important for interpretation than text. The context is Paul's general theology, and Schleiermacher's most characteristic uses of Romans 8 approach it on the basis of his understanding of that theology.

The contrast of law and gospel, as we have seen, is an essential key to Schleiermacher's treatment of Paul. In a sermon on Hebrews 10:8–12, Schleiermacher speaks of the link between the law and sin, and uses the idea of separation from the law as the context in which to understand Romans 8:1:

> Those who are sanctified, those who remain in the life which the Redeemer has kindled in them, grow and develop and separate themselves more and more from all share in sin and all trust in law and the work of the law. Among themselves they build each other up in the spiritual body of Christ. All who are sanctified are made perfect at one time through the sacrifice which he has presented. Their obedience, although in appearance always imperfect, is still an outflow of his perfect obedience, and is one with it....
>
> Thus, there is, as the Apostle Paul says, no condemnation for those who are in Christ Jesus, and we can thank God who has rescued us from this body of death, and given us the victory through our Lord Jesus Christ. (Rom. 8:1, 7:24, 25)[8]

In *The Christian Faith*, Schleiermacher speaks of the consciousness of freedom from sin, which in his thought is equivalent to freedom from law,

---

8. *Saemmtliche Werke*, part II, vol. 2 (*Vierte-Siebente Sammlung*), 173.

as based on the popular understanding of verse 2.⁹ Verse 3 he expounds in terms of the powerlessness of law to achieve the attainment of God's promises:

> If the Apostle is right in distinguishing the Law as, although a divine ordinance, yet something that came in between the promise to Abraham's seed and its fulfilment (Gal 3:19), and in asserting further that the Law lacks the power of the Spirit from which the Christian life must flow (Rom. 7:6 ff. and 8:3), then it cannot be maintained that the Law was inspired by the same Spirit of which the Apostle says that it is no longer communicated through the Law and its works (Gal 3:2), but God sends it into our hearts only through our connexion with Christ.[10]

This quotation shows not only Schleiermacher's contrast of law and gospel, but also his tendency to carry his interpretation beyond the meaning of the text. It is one thing to say, on the basis of these texts, that the law lacks the power of the Spirit to accomplish the promise of faith. It is quite another thing to draw the conclusion, as Schleiermacher does, that the spirit present in the Old Testament was not the one Holy Spirit which Christ has promised. One example of this extension of a text with a happy result occurs in one of the sermons on the Augsburg Confession, where he asserts that righteousness through faith belongs not to those who merely acknowledge Christ, but to those in whom Christ lives, and who live in Christ.[11] The text quoted is Romans 8:1, which speaks only of those who are in Christ, not of those in whom Christ lives. One may wonder why Schleiermacher does not cite Romans 8:10 or Colossians 1:27, 28 to confirm the connection between the concepts "Christ within" and "in Christ." An extension of meaning of a more questionable nature concerns Romans 8:2. In *The Christian Faith*, Schleiermacher cites this verse and Romans 7:25 to support his claim that the Christian can never have a consciousness of sin without at the same time being conscious of the power of redemption.[12] Such a remark owes less to Paul's text than it does to Schleiermacher's psychology.

The idea that in Christ there is no condemnation is explained, in one place, as a new aspect in the struggle between the flesh and the spirit, and in another, as the beginning of "the disappearance of the old man" in the

---

9. *Christian Faith*. vol. 1 (74:3), 311–12.

10. *Christian Faith*, vol. 2, (132:2), 608.

11. *Saemmtliche Werke*, part II, vol. 2 (*Vierte-Siebente Sammlung*), 662. See "On the Augsburg Confession IV."

12. *Christian Faith*, vol. 1 (66:2), 272–73.

removal of the consciousness of deserving punishment.[13] That only one who lacks such a consciousness of sin could be the Redeemer is given as an explanation of verse 2, although the connection seems remote.[14] Schleiermacher makes little comment on the contrast of flesh and Spirit in verses 4–8, merely remarking in a sermon that it is hard to think of a man setting himself against the truth, except under the influence of powerful bodily desire.[15] References to verse 9 and the following verses consist of vague comments on the presence of the Spirit within. Verse 9 and 1 Corinthians 12:3 are said to mean that "the presence of the Spirit . . . is the condition of anyone's sharing in the common life" an idea which is not contained in either text.[16] Verse 9, together with verse 11, is also interpreted as meaning that the action of the Spirit is internal.[17] This is a plausible inference, but it does not express the thought of the verses, and there is no evident connection between Paul's thought about the working of the Spirit and Schleiermacher's thought about the human self-consciousness as the locus of the work of the Spirit. The concept of Christ as the center of the consciousness is taken as expressing the meaning of the phrase "Christ in you" in verse 10, and this phrase is regarded as equivalent to the expression "led by the Spirit" in verse 14.[18]

Despite Schleiermacher's conception of Christ's resurrection being the prototype of our resurrection, he makes no reference to Romans 8:11 in this connection. In discussing adoption in *The Christian Faith*, he does not refer to verses 15 or 23, or, for that matter, to any New Testament passages at all.[19] Adoption is simply stated to be equivalent to forgiveness. In developing his doctrine of the Holy Spirit, Schleiermacher makes only inconsequential references to this chapter, and nowhere is the Spirit linked to his teaching on adoption or on the resurrection. The reference to verse 14 in the previous paragraph is the only reference which he makes to the section from verses 12–17.

In a sermon on Matthew 6:34, Schleiermacher comments on verses 18–23.[20] He speaks only of our yearning for something better, and makes no reference to the frustration of the whole creation. Our desire is for the full

13. *Saemmtliche Werke*, part II, vol. 2 (*Vierte-Siebente Sammlung*), 567; *The Christian Faith*, vol. 2 (101:2), 432–34.

14. *Christian Faith*, vol. 1 (68:3), 278–79.

15. *Saemmtliche Werke*, part II, vol. 2 (*Vierte-Siebente Sammlung*), 736.

16. *Christian Faith*, vol. 2 (121:2), 562–64.

17. *Christian Faith*, vol. 2 (123:2), 570–72.

18. *Christian Faith*, vol. 2 (100:1), 425–26, (124:2), 575–77.

19. *Christian Faith*, vol. 2 (109:2), 497–99, (111:4), 516–17. See also *Saemmtliche Werke*, part II, vol. 2 (*Vierte-Siebente Sammlung*), 176.

20. *Saemmtliche Werke*, part II, vol. 2 (*Vierte-Siebente Sammlung*), 13.

enjoyment of the privileges of sonship, for the complete revelation of the kingdom of God, and for the wider development of God's gracious decrees. This desire is closely linked, Schleiermacher says, to the work of redemption. In an uncharacteristic remark, he says that this longing is effective in human life even when it is unconscious. Our longing is not to be regarded as a curse of our life, but rather the circumstance from which arises the happiest and most blessed events of life. In another sermon, he cites verse 18 as one which causes someone who is suffering to seek a vision of the future life, as a help in dealing with present life.[21] In another, he speaks of the wealth of the fruits of righteousness as the goal of our striving, and that these fruits are offered to those who have surrendered claims to righteousness from the law and who have reached full perfection in faith in Jesus Christ.[22] The citations in this passage are to Galatians 2:19 and Romans 8:21 and 26. Just as striving after a better world cannot be regarded as a misfortune, so social and natural evil cannot be regarded as punishment for sin by the Christian. Schleiermacher makes this point in *The Christian Faith* as an explanation of the frustration of creation (v. 22), and of the afflictions which are powerless to separate us from Christ (vv. 35–39).[23] Sin is no genuine part of the new man in Christ, and despite his laboring against the aftereffects of former sin, and longing for the coming world, he does not have any remaining consciousness of guilt. The general striving for what is better is exemplified by Christian prayer, and Schleiermacher links this to verse 26 in a sermon.[24] We cannot properly pray for definite things, for all our particular prayers are dissolved in the general prayer given by the Spirit.

Schleiermacher's favorite in Romans 8 is verse 28: "We know that all things work together for good for those who love God, who are called according to his purpose." The first part of the verse is the text of one of his sermons, which has the title, "The Profitable Use of Public Disasters." In it, he remarks on the division among men, between those who receive God's blessing and those who do not. He says that none of us has the love of God as the sole effective influence in our lives:

> The comfort of Christianity is only for those whom God loves. In us it is the power of the divine will and of the Spirit himself. If you ask what is God's best gift which is to serve all in this way, I reply that it is not that this comfort itself may improve and be perfected, because what moves us to love God is already perfect.

---

21. *Saemmtliche Werke*, part II, vol. 4, (*Veroffentlichte Predigten*), 329.
22. *Saemmtliche Werke*, part II, vol. 2 (*Vierte-Siebente Sammlung*), 750.
23. *Christian Faith*, vol. 2 (109:2), 497–99.
24. *Saemmtliche Werke*, part II, vol. 3 (*Predigten*), 66.

God's best gift is that he will seize upon and make his own every earthly and human power in us, so that nothing else is effective or ordering in our lives, except him.[25]

On the basis of this introduction, which is all the use which he makes of the text, he sets out as the two points of the sermon the necessity for us to apprehend ourselves and to apprehend God. This sermon seems to be one of those preached in the period following Napoleon's conquest of Prussia in 1806. In one of his sermons from 1832, Schleiermacher repeats the argument that this verse means that God loves those whose whole habit of life is controlled by him, and that to these people, even disasters will serve a good purpose.[26] The sermon was preached on the occasion of public thanksgiving after a cholera epidemic in Berlin.

In another sermon of his later years, Schleiermacher maintains that God uses not only public disaster, but also our sinful action, to our profit.[27] In yet another sermon, this point is expanded to show that our weaknesses provide instruction and warning for our fellows, as theirs do for us.[28] God does not use our weaknesses simply for the building of our character, but, in respect to our whole lives, makes these weaknesses into strengths. This is part of his work in calling us and making us righteous (v. 30). In *The Christian Faith*, Schleiermacher's use of verse 28 is somewhat different. There, he cites it to support the points already made in reference to verse 22, that social and natural evil for the Christian are no longer connected with actual sin, nor are they to be regarded as punishment for sin.[29]

For Schleiermacher, justification is one of the two elements in regeneration; the other is conversion. In the process of regeneration, our sins are forgiven and we are recognized by God as his children. In developing these concepts in *The Christian Faith*, Schleiermacher cites verse 33 as evidence that the whole work of regeneration, both justification and conversion, is Christ's work.[30] It results in our sharing in the perfection and blessedness of Christ. The only citation of verse 34 is a confusing one in *The Christian Faith*, where Schleiermacher tries to link Christ's representation of us before God, his pleading of our case in heaven, with his work on earth.[31] Schleiermacher again seems concerned with the work of Christ as a whole

25. *Saemmtliche Werke*, part II, vol. 1 (*Erste-Dritte Sammlung*), 289.
26. *Saemmtliche Werke*, part II, vol. 4 (*Veroffentlichte Predigten*), 210.
27. *Saemmtliche Werke*, part II, vol. 2 (*Vierte-Siebente Sammlung*), 733.
28. *Saemmtliche Werke*, part II, vol. 2 (*Vierte-Siebente Sammlung*), 149.
29. *Christian Faith*, vol. 1 (84:2), 347–49; vol. 2 (104:4), 457–63.
30. *Christian Faith*, vol. 2 (109:3), 499–503.
31. *Christian Faith*, vol. 2 (104:5), 463–65.

personality, and, as before, it provides difficulties for exegesis and for theology. The final reference to Romans 8 is in a Christmas sermon on the meaning of the appearance of Christ.[32] Schleiermacher compares the weakness of the apostles with the greatness of the task which was given to them. He quotes 2 Corinthians 4:8–9 and Romans 8:35–39 to indicate the difficulties faced by the early church. It was Christ, who is God, who gave the power by which these and all other difficulties of the Christian life may be overcome.

This survey shows the fragmentary nature of Schleiermacher's consideration of Romans 8 in his sermons and doctrinal writing. Important sections of the chapter are omitted entirely, and they, together with other sections inadequately dealt with, fail to have a proper place in the formation of his theology. The conception of the renovation of nature is passed by, and no mention is made of this chapter in connection with the resurrection. Paul's teaching on the Christian hope receives scant treatment from Schleiermacher, and his comments on our yearning for something better cannot be regarded as an adequate use of the passages from this chapter on the subject. It has already been noted that Schleiermacher does not give this chapter a constructive place in the formation of his doctrine of the Holy Spirit. Also noted have been a number of instances in which Schleiermacher twists texts to arrive at conclusions which the passages do not warrant. Thus, one must conclude that his method of interpretation does every bit as much violence to the sense of biblical passages as does the citation of prooftexts which he despises. In both cases, the same difficulty arises: a meaning is assigned to a passage for dogmatic purposes which is not drawn from the passage itself. Schleiermacher recognizes the problem, but instead of his solution being a solution, it is just another illustration of the difficulty.

SCHLEIERMACHER'S USE OF SERMON TEXTS

A few additional remarks may be made concerning Schleiermacher's use of the Bible in his sermons. For his preaching, he used the Luther text of the Bible, apparently without reference to the Greek. An example of how this could affect the content of the sermon is provided by one of his sermons on the Christian household.[33] The text is Ephesians 6:1–3. In verse 1, Luther translates δίκαιον with the word *billig*. In this case, *billig* means "fitting" and is also used to translate δίκαιον in Philippians 1:7. The corresponding English translation would be "meet," which the King James Version uses for the Philippians passage. Schleiermacher expounds the passage as if "billig"

---

32. *Saemmtliche Werke*, part II, vol. 2 (*Vierte-Siebente Sammlung*), 81.
33. *Saemmtliche Werke*, part II, vol. 1 (*Erste-Dritte Sammlung*), 551.

means "profitable," as if Paul were commending obedience because it pays. Schleiermacher says that there is a sense in which we may let profitability order some of the smaller aspects of life, but that in higher things, righteousness must be the controlling principle.

This distinction would be quite impossible to mention with respect to this text for anyone who had the Greek word in mind. Sometimes the use of Luther's text adds to the immediate relevance of the sermon. Luther's text renders Matthew 6:34 as *Es ist genug, dass ein jeglicher Tag seine eigene Plage habe*. The use of *Plage* for κακία enables Schleiermacher to apply the text to the situation of Berlin, which was preparing itself for a cholera epidemic when he preached on the text in 1831.[34]

In his sermons, Schleiermacher makes virtually no reference to problems of text or translation. In a sermon from 1832, he mentions that Acts 8:37 is not part of the original text, and omits it from his reading of the passage.[35] In the *Homilies on John*, he passes chapter 8:1–11 without comment, but he does include John 7:53 in his reading and comments on it as part of the text.[36]

Schleiermacher's sermons are varied in their structure. Five volumes of them are devoted to continuous exposition of different books of the New Testament. More than seventy sermons deal with the first sixteen chapters of John's Gospel, the longest series in the group, preached over a four-year period from 1823 to 1826. Other series deal with Matthew and Mark, Acts, Colossians, and Philippians. The series on John consists of homilies in which Schleiermacher quotes a verse or phrase and then comments upon it. His method is to try to project the mind of John, and through him, the minds of Christ and of the other people who appear in the gospel. It is a homiletical example of his general hermeneutical approach. As we have seen in earlier chapters, Schleiermacher regards John's Gospel as an eyewitness account of most of the situations it records. Incidents are selected for inclusion in the gospel because they exhibit the dignity of Christ, and the developing conflict between him and the authorities. Schleiermacher seeks to reconstruct these situations, and then to understand the words in the context in which they were spoken. Examples of this have been cited in the discussion of the raising of Lazarus.[37] In some of the other expository sermons, the method is different. There is still the aim of reconstructing the original situation to which the text applies, but the major purpose is to outline a few points

---

34. *Saemmtliche Werke*, part II, vol. 2 (*Vierte-Siebente Sammlung*), 12.

35. *Saemmtliche Werke*, part II, vol. 3 (*Predigten*), 326.

36. *Saemmtliche Werke*, part II, vol. 9 (*Johannes*), 61, 65.

37. See ch. 4, "The Raising of Lazarus."

by which the text may be applied to Schleiermacher's hearers. Thus, in a sermon on Acts 8:36, 38, Schleiermacher recounts the story of the meeting of Philip and the Ethiopian eunuch as an example of how the gospel spread in the earliest times in the church, and as an example of how the contemporary Christian should make use of situations to spread the message about Christ.[38] The latter type of exposition is closer in form to Schleiermacher's general sermons. These are seldom expository in character. Some have a structure similar to the sermon on the Ethiopian eunuch: they reconstruct the original situation briefly in order to find a modern parallel. Thus, one of the sermons on the Augsburg Confession on 1 Peter 3:15 outlines what it meant in New Testament times to give an account of the Christian hope—what it meant at the time of the Reformation, and what it means in the present day.[39] Sometimes the points in the sermons are drawn from the texts; more frequently, one point is a theological comment on the text, and a second point is an application of this comment to the present. Some of the sermons, particularly those preached on Old Testament texts, make no attempt to understand the theological or historical context, but use the words from the Bible as if they were directly addressed to Schleiermacher's congregation. This approach is typical of his war sermons, such as the one which he preached in 1818 to commemorate the anniversary of the battle of Leipzig.[40] Verses 3 and 4 of Psalm 68 were used as expressions of joy at the allied victory over the armies of Napoleon.

Schleiermacher's sermons, like his dogmatic writings, illustrate the difficulty of isolating the source of his thought. In some cases, his use of Scripture in the sermons is arbitrary and lacking in conviction. In others, his use of his "divinatory" method of interpretation is a means of eliciting the intention of a passage so that it can really come alive for the faith of the hearers. Throughout the various uses of biblical passages which we have seen, certain aspects of his philosophy are apparent, and they color all of his exposition.

Nevertheless, Schleiermacher recognizes the need to expound the New Testament, and the greater part of what he has to say is derived from exposition, not from his general viewpoint of philosophy. His aim is to outline the contents of the New Testament without philosophical or dogmatic presuppositions. He fails to do this, but such a conclusion does not invalidate his approach; it merely means that, like other expositors of the

---

38. *Saemmtliche Werke*, part II, vol. 3 (*Predigten*), 326.

39. *Saemmtliche Werke*, part II, vol. 2 (*Vierte-Siebente Sammlung*), 626. See "On the Augsburg Confession II."

40. *Saemmtliche Werke*, part II, vol. 4 (*Veroffentlichte Predigten*), 77; *Selected Sermons*, 183.

Bible, he often finds his own ideas when he thinks he is discovering the mind of Paul or John.

8

The Problem of Authority

SCHLEIERMACHER'S REVOLUTIONARY APPROACH TO the interpretation of the Bible may be summarized by considering the locus of authority in his theology. Despite his emphasis on the church, and the importance which he gave to tradition, doctrine cannot be established on the authority of the church, nor is any interpretation of biblical passages established solely on the authority of the early Fathers or of any other received teaching. The Bible itself is not the authority for faith. Schleiermacher dismissed the Old Testament, and affirmed the New Testament as authentic and the sufficient norm of doctrine. This means that nothing in the New Testament is superfluous, and that it contains such material as is conducive to a right understanding and application of the gospel. Expressions of Christian faith subsequent to the New Testament must be compatible with it because the Holy Spirit, under whose influence the individual books were written and assembled as the canon, is still the source of these later expressions. The influence of the Holy Spirit now is the same as his influence in apostolic times. Thus, the normative character of the Scriptures rests on the unity and continued effectiveness of the Holy Spirit, rather than on the written word of the biblical text itself. The reversal of theological method in Schleiermacher's system rests on a reversal of the relationship between faith and the Scriptures, and this relationship rests on the interpretation given to teaching about the Holy Spirit in the New Testament.

THE REVERSAL OF METHOD

Schleiermacher's theological method reverses the relationship between faith and the Bible which had been found in traditional Protestantism:

> When we see the Bible, as it is often said, as the source of true faith, our opinion is not without error, for faith is older than the Bible. Certainly the Bible is the first witness to faith which has come to us. Faith in Christ arose from Christ himself, how he lived, spoke, and acted; and afterwards the Bible arose having originated in faith. Thus, Christ always remains the source of faith; he is now, and to this we must hold fast.[1]

This passage from one of Schleiermacher's sermons on the Augsburg Confession restates the burden of proposition 128 of *The Christian Faith* by denying the claim of traditional Protestantism that faith is based on the Scriptures. In *The Christian Faith*, this denial is extended by the proposition that faith is a prerequisite for *present acceptance* of the Bible, while in the sermon it is stated that faith is the prerequisite for the *production* of the Bible. Schleiermacher's explanations of his position deal first with the present demonstration of faith, and secondly with the historical reconstruction of the production of the New Testament.

Schleiermacher rejected all attempts to demonstrate faith. The use of the Scriptures "to compel faith" or "to force unbelievers into faith" was utterly perverted and doomed to failure.[2] If belief in Christ were to be based on Scripture, then the authority of Scripture must be based on some general principle of reason. This would imply that people of superior mind have an advantage with respect to faith, contrary to the basic principles of the Protestant churches. This is also the objection to any doctrine of inspiration contained within the New Testament itself: such a doctrine can be recognized only by someone who already has an adequate knowledge and understanding of the Bible, and thus it assumes an intellectual presupposition for faith. Schleiermacher maintains his point that faith is not knowledge, and does not depend upon knowledge. He expands this distinction to make a complete qualitative distinction between the acceptance of facts and the apprehension of faith. Evidence, whether from Scripture or from any other source, combined with rational deduction, could produce only an objective recognition of facts. This would be factual knowledge, and it has no

---

1. *Saemmtliche Werke*, part II, vol. 2 (*Vierte-Siebente Sammlung*), 632. See "On the Augsburg Confession II."
2. For this section, see *The Christian Faith*, vol. 1 (14), 70–76; vol. 2 (128:2), 592–93.

connection with a "true living fellowship with Christ."³ The best thing that an objective conviction of this kind can achieve is "to give an impulse towards the awakening of a fuller self-consciousness and towards the winning of a total impression of Christ; and only from this will faith then proceed."⁴ Schleiermacher here gives evidence of his epistemological dualism: objective knowledge refers to perceptible reality, whereas subjective feeling provides an intuition of spiritual reality, and there is no direct relationship between the one and the other. This is consistent with Schleiermacher's approach to other reputed evidences. The raising of Lazarus was a miracle witnessed by a group of people of various viewpoints. Each person gained the same objective knowledge of the event. Faith arose only in those who were already prepared for faith by inward disposition, and not in those who lacked this preparation. For the former, the miracle provided the occasion but not the proof of faith. Similarly, an objective acknowledgment of the dignity of the Bible might give an impulse toward faith, but it is not the ground of faith. On the contrary, such an objective acknowledgment really rests upon faith, even if this faith is at a very low stage of development.

This separation of objective knowledge and subjective intuition is the basis also for Schleiermacher's objection to the affirmation of the resurrection as doctrine. Christ rose from the dead and was seen by his disciples in a series of disconnected meetings. But the resurrection in this sense is a fact attested by the human senses: therefore, it cannot be an affirmation of faith. Faith is a perception of Christ's *spiritual* power and there can be no ground of faith derived from *sensible* perception. In one of his sermons on the raising of Lazarus, he affirms that there can be only one basis for faith:

> Always and forever there is but one ground for firm and living faith in our Lord and Redeemer, which he has offered and in which we may have life: this ground is none other than this, that we recognize in him the glory of the only-begotten Son of the Father, that we see in him his unity with the Father, so that we can derive no viewpoint from all his speech and actions, all his words and deeds, other than that of his Father and our Father in heaven.⁵

Faith and knowledge of facts are always to be separated: faith and doctrine are not to be confused. The failure to recognize these distinctions, in Schleiermacher's view, is a persistent source of error in Christian understanding.

---

3. *Christian Faith*, vol. 2 (128:1), 591–92; *The Christian Faith*, vol. 1 (14), 70–76.
4. *Christian Faith*, vol. 1 (14), 76.
5. *Saemmtliche Werke*, part II, vol. 9 (*Johannes*), 282, sermon on John 11:41–54.

Schleiermacher's rejection of evidences for faith is the basis on which he affirms that faith is the prerequisite for the acceptance of the Bible in the present time. He has a second explanation, which deals with the reason faith was a prerequisite for the production of the New Testament books in apostolic times. This is an application of his own hermeneutical method to the understanding of the New Testament—through reconstruction of the process through which its books were written and gathered together. Each of the books individually was written for some special purpose within the early church. The letters of Paul were written to particular congregations and were relevant to local circumstances of life and doctrine. The doctrinal teaching was presented in a way that related Paul's own consciousness of faith to the strengths and weaknesses of doctrine among the people whom he was addressing. The historical books were written by Christians of the second generation to provide material for preaching which could take the place of personal memories of Christ on the part of his original followers. Each individual book, and the collection of the New Testament as a whole, is to be regarded as a work of the church giving witness to Christ. Such witness is a testimony to the experience of its author, and its purpose is to arouse in others a similar experience. The peculiar character of the New Testament rests upon the fact that its authors and compilers were part of the apostolic circle, in which the living fellowship with Christ provided an impulse of sufficient power to overcome the destructive influences of alien thought. Membership in this circle was confined to those who had attached themselves to Christ, because their religious self-consciousness had, under his influence, convinced them of their need for redemption. They were also assured in themselves of Christ's redeeming power. It was only in the strength of this assurance that they were able to present Christ to others. This assurance is also the faith which Schleiermacher regards as the prerequisite for the original writing of the New Testament. In his view, faith is "the certainty that the influence of Christ puts an end to the state of being in need of redemption."[6] Thus, just as faith is needed for the present acceptance of the New Testament, so was it needed by those who wrote the books which comprise it. Both the writing and the reading of the Bible presuppose faith; faith does not presuppose the reading of the Bible.

The consideration of this reversal of method in approaching the Bible leads to a consideration of Schleiermacher's conception of inspiration.[7] He denies the traditional concept that the biblical authors were mere stenographers writing at the dictation of a mysterious voice from beyond. In

6. *Christian Faith*, vol. 1 (14:1), 68–69.
7. *Christian Faith*, vol. 2 (130), 597.

his view, the writers were guided by the Holy Spirit as part of the general guidance which directed the whole life of the church. The teaching which they transmitted is derived from Christ, and thus the whole of the New Testament is to be regarded as a gift from him. Each individual presentation of this teaching is mixed with material derived from other sources, and the work of the Holy Spirit in the early church was the work of separating purer material from the less pure, and designating certain material as *canonical* and other material as *apocryphal*. This process was at work in the writing and editing of the individual books, and in the gathering of the canon. The apostles were those men in whom the action of the Spirit was most profound, and in whom faith expressed itself as a keener intention to let the Spirit be the exclusive rule of their lives. It is from this circle that the New Testament writings proceed, and the inspiration which we attribute to the Bible is simply the leading of the Holy Spirit, which is evident in the entire lives of these men. Their writing and speech is to be viewed as the transmission of the divine revelation, which was Christ.

Schleiermacher recognizes two passages as specially relevant to the idea of the inspiration of the Scriptures: 2 Timothy 3:16 ("All Scripture is inspired by God and is useful") and 2 Peter 1:21 ("No prophecy ever came by human will, but men and women moved by the Holy Spirit spoke from God"). Both passages refer to the books of the Old Testament. The former passage has been interpreted in the sense that inspiration applied to the act of writing on the part of the authors, quite apart from the rest of their lives. The latter passage is completely open to the interpretation that this inspiration affected all their actions, and applied to the written material only in the setting of an inspired life. There is no warrant in either passage, or elsewhere, for interpreting them as meaning that the biblical writers were provided with special information, by way of inspiration, which they recorded under the Spirit's leading. In any case, as Schleiermacher concludes in several instances, it is not correct to speak of activity of the Holy Spirit prior to Christ, and hence the inspiration of the Old Testament cannot be referred to the same Christian Spirit whose work is seen in the New Testament. Thus, the two passages in question are not strictly relevant to a discussion of the inspiration of the New Testament, and the doctrine of inspiration cannot be regarded as a strictly scriptural doctrine.

Properly applied, the term "inspiration" refers to the apostolic period in the life of the church, and to the apostolic class of people whom the Spirit guided in the transmission of the revelation in Christ:

> The peculiar inspiration of the Apostles is not something that belongs exclusively to the books of the New Testament. These

books only share it; and inspiration in this narrower sense, conditioned as it is by the purity and completeness of the apostolic grasp of Christianity, covers the whole of the official apostolic activity thence derived. If we consider the inspiration of Scripture in this context as a special portion of the official life of the Apostles which in general was guided by inspiration, we shall hardly need to raise all those difficult questions about the extent of inspiration.[8]

Schleiermacher's rejection of the traditional concept of inspiration is similar to his rejection of the traditional relationship of faith and Scripture. Both rest on the same two arguments. First, the traditional doctrine contains a rationalistic presupposition which is contrary to a proper understanding of faith. Throughout his theology, Schleiermacher tended to emphasize those aspects of faith which were noncognitive and nonintellectual. Secondly, the traditional doctrine misrepresented the actual process by which the Scriptures came to be written. The New Testament was written and gathered under the guidance of the Holy Spirit, and the Spirit is to be seen as the common life of the Christian community, a life which was founded by Christ. Thus, it is the doctrine of the Holy Spirit which lies at the foundation of Schleiermacher's theological revolution. The authority which the Bible possesses is a derivative authority and rests upon the foundation of the work of the Spirit. Yet the work of the Spirit cannot be arbitrary and free from the Scriptures; it is intimately connected with the witness which is borne by the Scriptures. It is necessary to consider Schleiermacher's doctrine of the Holy Spirit to understand this connection and find the locus of authority both for the Spirit and for the Scriptures.

THE DOCTRINE OF THE HOLY SPIRIT

Schleiermacher defines the Holy Spirit as "the common Spirit of the new corporate life founded by Christ."[9] In the Christian community, there is a new life, shared by all its members, which expresses itself as work toward a common goal. The character of Christianity is marked by the quality of fellowship, in which every individual is a constituent part. The life of every individual is determined by this common life and common will for the kingdom of God. The perfection of the church is the approach to the kingdom of God in which the common bonds between the various individuals and groups within the church are drawn closer and closer together. The common

8. *Christian Faith*, vol. 2 (130:2), 599–600.
9. *Christian Faith*, vol. 2 (121), 560.

tendency of all members of the fellowship toward a shared life constitutes a moral personality, based on the love which each individual feels for other members of the community, in its turn based on common love for Christ. The fellowship is animated by a common spirit which moves in all the expressions of common life, and this is the Holy Spirit. Schleiermacher claims that his conception of the Holy Spirit is a correct interpretation of the teaching of the New Testament, and that it appears strange because most dogmatic systems base their teaching about the Spirit on the doctrine of the Trinity, which Schleiermacher considers as a secondary and artificial doctrine. His concept of the biblical teaching about the Spirit may be summarized in a few propositions. The Holy Spirit is a unifying Spirit drawing together in a common life all Christians and all sections of the Christian church. The Spirit is given to the assembled community, and within this community, various gifts are given to individuals. These gifts are not contrary to one another, but are complementary, so that all who are part of the church live a life of fellowship and mutual cooperation. The origin of the Spirit is in Christ, so that all of these gifts have Christ as their source, and nothing can be seen as a true gift of the Spirit apart from Christ's name and teaching. The Holy Spirit is given by Christ, and is only fully transmitted after his departure from his followers. The work of the Spirit among Christians is the continuation of Christ's work on earth. All fellowship with Christ is the work of the Holy Spirit, and without the Spirit, Christ is not truly known, nor is his work done. The basis of these statements will be discussed briefly.

In a sermon about Pentecost, Schleiermacher says that the continuing effect of the divine Spirit, now, as in the early church, is that believers devote themselves to the teaching and fellowship of the apostles.[10] This is based on Acts 2:42: "they devoted themselves to the apostles' teaching and fellowship, to the breaking of bread and the prayers."

He asserts that the fellowship of the apostles exists in every branch of the church, wherever people gather in Christ's name, wherever people confess their need of redemption and receive forgiveness in the name of Jesus. In the early days of Christianity, this constituted a single fellowship in a single place, gathered together for teaching, for the sacraments, and for prayer. In principle, this is still the case, and from a spiritual viewpoint there is still only one fellowship, which includes not only all Christians in the contemporary world, but all believers of the past and the present. The work of the Holy Spirit is to unify, strengthen, and extend this fellowship, and this includes the work of recognizing and sharing in the life or other Christian bodies in a spirit of brotherly love. The aim of the Spirit is to bring

---

10. *Saemmtliche Werke*, part II, vol. 2 (*Vierte-Siebente Sammlung*), 216.

all men into the fellowship of Christ and to gather all Christians into a single community. Thus, the Holy Spirit is the Spirit of unity and love, and is given to the community as a whole. In *The Christian Faith*, Schleiermacher cites John 20:22 as evidence that the Spirit is given to a group of people, and that by this gift they are transformed into an organic whole, with a common activity and a common will.[11]

Within the life of fellowship, the one Spirit gives differing gifts, which lead people in various directions. In the sermon just mentioned, Schleiermacher remarks on the differing viewpoints and expressions, the differing kinds of Christian piety which may arise from the single Spirit. He likens the varied forms of Christian life to a vast choir, and each individual hears that part of the choir's song which is relevant to his need and his service. But in all the variety, there is a common direction supplied by the Spirit, so that each particular life and gift is guided by the entire fellowship. The work of the individual and of the community is not to be seen in narrow terms, as talk about the word of God, or as mutual edification, but includes the whole life in which faith is expressed. In a sermon on 1 Corinthians 12:31 ("But strive for the greater gifts. And I will show you a still more excellent way"), Schleiermacher identifies the highest gift of the Spirit as Christian teaching, and the more excellent way of which Paul speaks as the love which animates the Christian fellowship.[12] This love is not to be expressed only in works of piety, but in daily living; there must be no false separation of what is worldly and what is spiritual. Instead, the work of love should extend into the life of the home, into business, into social life, and into our lives as citizens. Schleiermacher's discussion of inspiration with respect to the Scriptures may be regarded as a particular application of this aspect of his doctrine of the Holy Spirit. The apostles were led by the Spirit in their Christian teaching, and thus they were the recipients of the highest of the Spirit's gifts. Because of this gift, and their own close association with Christ, they were able to formulate Christian teaching in a way which is the standard for all subsequent expressions of faith.

The source of all the gifts of the Spirit is Jesus Christ. This seemingly innocuous statement is interpreted by Schleiermacher in a way which sums up the revolutionary aspect of his whole theology. The Holy Spirit is the gift of the Christ during and after his earthly ministry, and the teaching of the Spirit is to be traced to Christ's words. Hence, there can have been no work of the Spirit prior to Christ's manhood, and no work of the Spirit outside of the church. In *The Christian Faith*, Schleiermacher adduces Christ's promises of the Holy Spirit of truth from John's Gospel (John 14:16, 17; 16:7-14)

---

11. *Christian Faith*, vol. 2 (121:2), 562-64.
12. *Saemmtliche Werke*, part II, vol. 2 (*Vierte-Siebente Sammlung*), 532-48.

as testimony that Christ made no reference to an earlier gift of the Spirit.[13] In one of his homilies, he quotes from John 14:25, 30 and 26:

> I have said these things to you while I am still with you.... I will no longer talk much with you.... But the Advocate, the Holy Spirit, whom the Father will send in my name, will teach you everything, and remind you of all that I have said to you.

He comments as follows:

> It appears that this latter verse implies that the Spirit of God would confirm for them in their inner disposition, all that they had already heard from the Redeemer. But the former seems to imply that he would communicate to them in addition things that the Redeemer himself had not yet been able to say.
>
> As far as this latter idea is concerned we must understand the words of the Lord with greater circumspection and caution. We must compare everything which he otherwise said about the work of the divine Spirit among his disciples . . . with these words, so that we may not follow a dangerous false trail. For it could appear, from these words considered by themselves, as if thoughts could arise in the souls of men through the divine Spirit, without connection to what the Redeemer himself had previously spoken on earth to his disciples, and about which we can be assured, that we possess at least what is essential in the recorded speech of the Lord. This has misled many otherwise well-meaning and pious minds in all periods of the Christian church, many dispositions whose thought undoubtedly is directed toward God. Yet it is very far removed from the original truth of the gospel, which nevertheless is to be regarded as the inspiration of the divine Spirit. Yes, it has even misled human reason, which is bold and trusts itself too much, in that it has regarded itself as one with the divine Spirit, and regarded everything which stems from it as divine, whether it agrees with the words of the Lord or not. Neither the one nor the other was the meaning of the Lord, and we wish to hold fast to the original belief set forth from the beginning in our church, that the Spirit of God effects nothing among us except through the Word, and that we may not ascribe anything to him unless we become conscious in our minds that it agrees with what we ourselves know to be the Word of the Lord.[14]

---

13. *Christian Faith*, vol. 2 (123:1), 569–70.
14. *Saemmtliche Werke*, part II, vol. 9 (*Johannes*), 459–60, sermon on John 14:25–31.

The implications of this are very far-reaching. It means that the work of the Holy Spirit is not to be seen in the Old Testament, in rationalistic or idealistic philosophy, or in formulations of Christian doctrine which are based on either of these sources. Thus, the Holy Spirit has no part in the original creation of the world or in the events of Jewish history.[15] The Hebrew prophets expressed the common spirit of Jewish theocracy, but not the Christian Spirit which stems from the life and words of Jesus. The Holy Spirit had no part in the birth of Jesus, for it was only with his teaching ministry that the work of the Spirit was first expressed in an elementary way. It can be seen that Schleiermacher's whole theology of the Old Testament is based on this concept of the Spirit, as is his interpretation of Paul's teaching on the contrast of law and gospel, works and faith. His evaluation of the doctrine of the Trinity is drawn from the same source. There are thus three characteristics of the work of the Spirit which must all be observed in the service of correct interpretation: the work of the Spirit is subsequent in time to the coming of the Redeemer and is found in the community which preserves his memory; the teaching of the Spirit interprets the specific words of the Lord as they were recorded by his followers; consciousness of the Spirit depends on the conscious recognition of the name and the proclamation of Christ. Where one of these characteristics is missing, there can be no recognized work of the Holy Spirit in a proper sense.

Schleiermacher recognizes the common spirit among the disciples during Christ's life as a kind of intimation of the Spirit, but the true outpouring of the Spirit occurred at Pentecost, which was the beginning of his work within the Christian church as such.[16] Only at that time was the gift of the Spirit fully communicated and received. Only in the absence of Christ could his disciples be stirred up to free spontaneous activity in his name. The gift of the Spirit was given to believers, and since Pentecost it has only been believers to whom the Spirit has been given. The work of the Spirit among Christians is the continuation of the activity of Christ. In the sermon just quoted, Schleiermacher interprets Galatians 2:20 in the sense that Christ lives on in the community of believers, and in the lives of individual believers. In principle, his work is perfect and complete, but the carrying forth of that work to every land and every human being is barely begun in his own ministry. This is the task assigned to the church.

Just as one cannot speak of the work of the Holy Spirit unless that work is referred to the Redeemer, so one cannot acknowledge the lordship

---

15. *Christian Faith*, vol. 2 (123:1), 569–70.
16. *Christian Faith*, vol. 2 (122:1), 565–66.

of Christ apart from the impulse of the Holy Spirit.[17] In *The Christian Faith*, Schleiermacher refers to 1 Corinthians 12:3 as the basis of this idea: "No one can say 'Jesus is Lord' except by the Holy Spirit." The indwelling of the Holy Spirit is a prerequisite for living fellowship with Christ. This means that the Holy Spirit has an essential part in the work of redemption, which is the creation in us of the will to assume God as the active principle of our lives. It is the indwelling of the Holy Spirit which makes us conscious of the fact that we are the children of God and that Jesus Christ is our Lord. To be led by the Spirit and to have the life of Christ within us signify both our status as children of God and as members of the Christian church. All the gifts which God gives for strength and service within the church are dependent upon the Spirit, and these gifts can only be exercised within the believers, sharing in the gifts of the Holy Spirit, and living in fellowship with Christ. The Holy Spirit within us is a powerful impulse which determines our whole personality, but works only in connection with our memory and understanding of Christ's life and teaching. The importance of the words of Christ is summed up in Schleiermacher's comment on John 16:13–14:

> The Spirit of God in the hearts of the disciples ought to be a continuous hearing, a continuous attending to what the Lord himself had said to them when he was with them. For these phrases belong together: "He will take what is mine and declare it to you," and "Whatever he hears he will speak." The steadfast maintenance, the life-giving preservation of what the Lord has spoken, would become among them the power of a mature proclamation of the grace and mercy of God in Christ Jesus.[18]

THE PROCLAMATION OF CHRIST

All Christian gifts are to be traced to the work of the Holy Spirit. His is the impulse which leads to faith. From him comes fellowship with the Redeemer and with the believing community. In him is shaped the new Christian personality in which the individual hears the gospel in his own language and in accordance with his own need, and by the power of the Spirit he responds accordingly. The highest gift of the Spirit is Christian teaching or doctrine, and the office of teaching in the church is exercised under the guidance of the Spirit for the strengthening and extending of the Christian fellowship. Hence, it may be said that the doctrinal authority for

---

17. *Christian Faith*, vol. 2 (124:1), 574–75.
18. *Saemmtliche Werke*, part II, vol. 9 (*Johannes*), 521, sermon on John 16:4–15.

Schleiermacher is found in the Holy Spirit. However, as we have seen, this authority cannot be separated from the witness of the Scriptures. Both the Scriptures themselves and the Holy Spirit carry out their function by reliance on the speech of Christ, and it is here that we may find the true locus of theological authority in Schleiermacher's system.

The importance of preaching, in Schleiermacher's thought, cannot be overemphasized. All preaching traces itself back to the original self-proclamation of Christ, and this was the distinctive beginning of Christianity. Since that time, Christianity has spread itself by no other means than that of preaching. This concept of preaching is outlined in the introduction to *The Christian Faith*,[19] and it is given, for its general sense, the widest possible meaning. It is every type of expression of the Christian self-consciousness, and every type of language of faith. In his consideration of religious language, Schleiermacher breaks down the general concept into types of speech: poetical, rhetorical, and didactic. Sermons, as they are regularly delivered, are to be regarded as rhetorical speech. But the general concept of preaching is much wider; it includes all of these categories and every proposition which bears witness to the determination of the religious self-consciousness. Thus, all ecclesiastical doctrine is preaching, and so is the New Testament itself.

In the light of this concept of proclamation, Schleiermacher's own work is to be seen in a distinctive setting. His life's work was to be a preacher, and in his later years, he concentrated more and more on this task. Numerous interpreters of his work regard his preaching as a secondary activity, finding the center of his thought in such widely diverse areas as mystical philosophy and nationalistic politics; such interpretations are entirely inadequate. Within the broader concept of preaching, all his writings on theology are to be included, along with the sermons delivered from a pulpit. Even within the narrower designation of rhetorical speech, the sermons occupy one-third of the volumes, and these from a man who believed that sermons were to be heard and not read. He was very reluctant to publish his sermons, and many must have been lost. In addition to the sermons, a good case could be advanced for including *Addresses on Religion* among the rhetorical rather than the doctrinal works. It is clear that when *Addresses* was written, it was read as a document directed to arousing attention, rather than as a scientific treatise. In fine, Schleiermacher ought to be regarded as a Christian preacher, not one with whom all Christians would be content, but nevertheless one who had the highest respect for the preaching office.

It is within the category of proclamation that the interpretation of the Bible is to be pursued. The material of the New Testament is not primarily

---

19. *Christian Faith*, vol. 1 (15), 76–78; see also (16), 78–83, (18), 85–88.

doctrinal in character. Doctrinal language is didactic, a derivative and secondary form of speech which collates and systematizes the expressions which arise in poetical and rhetorical speech. The latter are the direct and original forms of religious self-expression, and present a direct response to a moment of exaltation or an attempt to arouse such a response in others. The New Testament writings are the supreme example of the use of speech within the church to communicate the Christian consciousness of God. But like all human communication, they can only speak of God as he is known in relation to us. Thus, the language of the Bible is human language which shares the limited characteristics of all human concepts. It is not adequate to speak of God as he is in himself, for any such concept could be neither expressed nor understood. The Scriptures share with other forms of human communication certain characteristics which are valid and relevant only within the circle for which the individual book was written. All the books contain material which is incidental, and bound in its expression to the knowledge and concepts current in apostolic times. But they are uniquely suitable to bear witness to the life and teaching of Christ, and by means of this witness, to evoke in others a similar witness. Thus, they are the first member in the series of writings which are designated as part of "the ministry of the Word"[20] within the church, and which are indispensable for the life of the church. It is because the New Testament is proclamation that Christians subsequent to the apostolic period have been able to base their faith upon the same ground which was the ground of faith for the first disciples themselves.

The dignity of the preaching office within the church, and the unique honour with which the Scriptures are regarded, both rest on the character which they possess as proclamation, as witness-bearing to the redemptive work of Christ. Proclamation is one of the unvarying features of the church, whose origin is found in Christ himself and whose continuing function is to present Christ to men. It is the origin of preaching which provides the central authority for all humanity and all doctrine. Schleiermacher refers to Christ's own preaching as the starting point of everything within Christianity. From that preaching springs the faith of the original disciples. Every emotion within the Christian self-consciousness is awakened by this original self-proclamation. Its content is the content of the apostles' own preaching, and, as we have seen, the teaching of the Holy Spirit is confined to the confirmation of what was said by Christ. All doctrine is to be judged by its standard; every expression of Christian preaching must be based on its spirit. Schleiermacher's concept of preaching is summed up as follows:

---

20. *Christian Faith*, vol. 2 (127), 591.

> The whole work of the Redeemer Himself was conditioned by the communicability of his self-consciousness by means of speech, and similarly Christianity has always and everywhere spread itself solely by preaching.[21]

The continuing function of preaching is to communicate the total impression of Christ's being, in order to evoke in others the sense of the need for redemption and of the assurance of redemption in Christ. It always takes the form of testimony to the speaker's own personal experience, and by this means seeks to evoke the same experience in others. But in every case, its content is to be traced back to the view of Christ given in Scripture, and anything individual in its presentation must be a legitimate development of Scripture. Preaching in the church is the sole means by which the will of God and his love for humanity are communicated. But "preaching" is a term of very wide meaning:

> Everything that the individual or a community can do by word or deed for the extension of the kingdom of God, being a continuation of, and therefore included in, the prophetic activity of Christ, may be summed up in the terms 'proclamation' or 'preaching.' And preaching, in this meaning and compass, springs from, and is the natural utterance for, faith.[22]

Thus, the whole work of the Christian community, expressive of its faith founded upon Scripture, is gospel proclamation, and not just formal preaching within the setting of worship. All teaching in the community goes back to Christ and is the progressive unfolding of his original preaching.

This is how Schleiermacher conceives of his own doctrinal system: it is an exposition of the *teaching* of Christ. The teaching of Christ is an essential part of his redeeming work, and rests on the new and unique revelation of God in him. The essence of this teaching can be summarized in three parts: the doctrine of his person, the doctrine of his work and the doctrine of his relationship to the Father. The essential interpretation of the Bible is to be found in terms of Christ's perfection of humanity, the existence of God within him, and the communication of eternal life through the continuation of the proclamation of Christ. Faith is founded upon preaching, and all preaching in founded upon Christ's commission, upon his own self-proclamation. Thus, the source of teaching, the authority for doctrine, and the true interpretation of the Bible are all to be found in Christ's original presentation of himself to humanity.

21. *Christian Faith*, vol. 1 (15:2), 77–78.
22. *Christian Faith*, vol. 2 (120:2), 553–55.

Conclusions

MANY ASPECTS OF SCHLEIERMACHER'S system are elusive in expression. Many examples can be found in which he makes a statement whose implications are very extensive, yet which is qualified in such a way that these consequences are altered or avoided. It is easy to give undue weight to one aspect of his thought by failing to note the qualification, or else by failing to relate it to some other aspect of his system. The conclusions of this study differ from those of some other interpreters of Schleiermacher, because they rely on some of his writings which are seldom read. The present conclusions are not put forward as a claim to settle the many disputed points with respect to Schleiermacher's theology, but only as a presentation of aspects of his thought which are seldom considered. It is hoped that the investigation may be continued farther and that a wider series of questions may be raised with respect to his interpretation.

1. In his interpretation of the Bible, Schleiermacher maintains one foot in each of two camps. On the one hand, he is the philosopher approaching the Bible with a free hand to accept, reject, or reshape ideas in accordance with his own predilections; many biblical concepts disappear entirely in the process. On the other hand, he is the Christian preacher determined at all costs to bear witness to the unsurpassable dignity of the person and work of Christ. Christ is the *given* of faith, and apart from his name and teaching, nothing is of value to the Christian life.

2. Schleiermacher affirms the historical character of the person and life of Christ as strongly as he can. In his view, the historical evidence could hardly be better. It consists of a historical chain of witnesses from one generation to another, passing on their impressions and their convictions about him. This chain of personal witness is backed by documents written by a variety of people for a variety of people, but all

expressing a common witness to the most important facts of Christ's life. Schleiermacher puts extraordinary reliance upon certain details from the Gospels as accurate reports of what Jesus said and did. Yet some historical aspects of Christ's life are entirely ignored.

3. For Schleiermacher, the historic witness to faith in Christ is even stronger than the witness to historical fact. Christ is even stronger than the witness to historical fact. Personal witness to Christian faith is an aspect of the work of the Holy Spirit, and it is the assurance of the Spirit that current expressions of the religious self-consciousness cannot run contrary to the God-consciousness expressed by the biblical writers. However, the weaknesses of Schleiermacher's position are clearly visible at this point. Schleiermacher deliberately sets his theological system contrary to received teaching on a great number of Christian doctrines. One must wonder if the Holy Spirit really was at work in both early and later periods, whether the one Spirit of truth allowed for such variety and outright contradiction between the thought of one period and that of another. Schleiermacher employs a very convenient device in drawing his doctrine of the Holy Spirit from John 14–16: he simply dismisses conflicting passages as references to another spirit, and conflicting doctrines as the product of philosophical speculation. It seems that only the disciple John and Schleiermacher together had a right understanding of the Spirit.

4. The difference between the Old and the New Testaments, which represents the central problem in Schleiermacher's interpretation of the Bible, depends upon his doctrine of the Spirit. The Holy Spirit is the common spirit of a human fellowship, existing in the consciousness of members of that fellowship. The distinctive mark of the Holy Spirit which differentiates it from all natural spirits within human life is the name and teaching of the Redeemer. Hence, Schleiermacher cannot retain the Old Testament in his positive concept of the word of God. In the Old Testament, there is no explicit recognition of Jesus of Nazareth. If Schleiermacher were to accept the Old Testament, he would have to affirm the work of the Spirit apart from the name of Christ, and this would mean that the often-repeated charge against Schleiermacher was true: the Holy Spirit would be identical with the general spirit of humanity.

5. For Schleiermacher, the Holy Spirit is not identical with the general spirit of humanity, and therefore it is a mistake to regard his theology as a development of the single principle of human self-awareness. His interpretation of the New Testament shows that there is no one

principle, whether psychological or philosophical, which can be regarded as the unique center of his thought. His philosophical ideas have a strong influence upon his biblical exegesis at a number of points, but his exposition of Scripture is no mere spinning out of a speculative worldview. Exposition is part of the church's task of bearing witness to Christ, under the influence of the Holy Spirit.

6. The Bible is to be interpreted as the normative example of witness to Christian faith. It is written in human language, and its words and expressions gain their meaning from the normal usage of human speech. Thus, the Bible requires to be interpreted in the same way in which all other human communication is interpreted. But Christian faith is the response to God's self-communication by means of human speech, and the New Testament is the unique witness to this communication; by it, all subsequent response is to be shaped. God's communication of himself to human beings is achieved through proclamation, and all such proclamation is based upon the words and the person of Jesus Christ. The Bible is the witness to Jesus Christ, because in the New Testament is to be found the authentic record of Christ's presentation of himself. Schleiermacher's interpretation of the Bible is thus seen to be his own response to the original self-proclamation of Christ, through which God communicates with humanity.

Concluding Unscientific Postscript, 2021

SCHLEIERMACHER'S USE OF HIS OWN HERMENEUTIC

Schleiermacher centered his understanding of the New Testament on John's Gospel, and the teaching of Paul. Among the Epistles, he regarded Romans, Galatians, First Thessalonians, and First and Second Corinthians as central in Paul's teaching. Along with these five, he placed special emphasis on Colossians. The article on Colossians 1:15–20 is the ground for his rejection of the Old Testament in Christian teaching: Jesus Christ, as Son of God, had no connection with the origin of human life, or the world itself. This is Schleiermacher's interpretation of Paul's teaching in this letter. Would it have been Schleiermacher's teaching in the five letters which are central to St. Paul?

Hermeneutics, according to Schleiermacher, is the discipline of understanding correctly another person's speech and writing. Understanding is not just knowing the definition of words, it also depends on knowing the person who used those words. This is not a mechanical act, but rather what Schleiermacher called "divinatory."

In dealing with the New Testament Gospels, Schleiermacher considered that John's Gospel was the record of an eyewitness, and Schleiermacher would have intended to grasp the personality of the author as well as his words. What about the letters of Paul? In dealing with the five special epistles there may have been the same intention. Colossians receives a different emphasis. How is detailed grammatical analysis to be coordinated with the personality of the author of Romans?

In his preaching, Schleiermacher was capable of quoting passages in contexts which had no real connection with the original biblical text.

All preachers do this, and Schleiermacher was no exception. Theologians do the same. How is a text to be understood? How does understanding itself occur? Schleiermacher's hermeneutic raises these issues, but does not solve them.

Selected Bibliography

The bibliography prepared by Terrence N. Tice on Schleiermacher's writings and subsequent literature is an indispensable reference for any critical discussion of his work and influence. See the notation below under *Schleiermacher Bibliography*.

WORKS BY FRIEDRICH SCHLEIERMACHER

Friedrich Schleiermachers saemmtliche Werke. 31 vols. Berlin: G. Reimer, 1834–64.

Abteilung I: Theologie

1. *Kurze Darstellung des theologischen Studiums Ueber die Religion*, 1843.
2. *Ueber die Schriften des Lukas | Ueber den sogenannten ersten Brief des Paulos an den Timotheus*, 1836.

   Ueber Kolosser 1:15-20, 1836.

   Ueber seine Glaubenslehre an Herrn Dr. Luecke, 1836.
5. *Vermischte Schriften Ueber den eigenthuemlichen Werth und das bindende Ansehen symbolischer Buecher*, 1846.
7. *Hermeneutik und Kritik mit besonderer Beziehung auf das Neue Testament*, 1838.
8. *Einleitung ins neue Testament*, 1845.
12. *Die christliche Sitte*, 1843.

Abteilung II: Predigten

1. *Erste-Dritte Sammlung*, 1843.
2. 8,9 *Ueber das Evangelium des Johannes*, 1837, 1847.
3. *Veroffentlichte Predigten*, 1844.
4. *Vierte-Siebente Sammlung*, 1843.

Abteilung III: Philosophie

1. *Reden und Abhandlungen*, 1835.
2. *Ueber den Unterschied swischen Naturgesez und Sittengesez*

———. *Aus Schleiermachers Leben in Briefen.* 4 vols. Edited by Ludwig Jonas and Wilhelm Dilthey. Berlin, 1858–63.
———. *Brief Outline on the Study of Theology.* Translated by Terrence N. Tice. Richmond, VA: John Knox, 1966.
———. *The Christian Faith.* Edited by H. R. Mackintosh and J. S. Stewart. Edinburgh: T. & T. Clark, 1928.
———. *The Christian Faith.* Edited by Richard Niebuhr. New York: Harper & Row, 1963.
———. *Der christliche Glaube, nach den Grundsaetzen der evangelischen Kirche in Zusammenhange dargestellt.* 2 vols. 2nd ed. Berlin: 1830–31.
———. *Christmas Eve, Dialogue on the Incarnation.* Translated by Terrence N. Tice. Richmond, VA: John Knox, 1967.
———. *Hermeneutics: The Handwritten Manuscripts.* Edited by Heina Kimmerle. Translated by James Duke and Jack Forstman. American Academy of Religion. Atlanta: Scholars, 1986.
———. *The Life of Schleiermacher as Unfolded in His Autobiography and Letters.* 2 vols. Translated by Frederica Rowan. London: Smith, Elder, 1860.
———. *On Religion: Speeches to Its Cultured Despisers.* Translated by John Oman. New York: Harper & Row, 1958.
———. *On Religion: Speeches to Its Cultured Despisers.* Translated by Richard Crouter. Cambridge: Cambridge University Press, 1996.
———. *On the Doctrine of Election, with Special Reference to the Aphorisms of Dr. Bretschneider.* Translated by Iain G. Nicol and Allen G. Jorgenson. Columbia Series in Reformed Theology. Louisville: Westminster John Knox, 2012.
———. *Predigten.* 5 vols. in 4. Berlin: Eugen Grosser, 1873–77.
———. *Selected Sermons of Schleiermacher.* Translated by Mary F. Wilson. London: Hodder & Stoughton, 1890.
———. *Ueber die Religion: Reden an die Gebildeten unter ihren Veraechtern.* Vol. 255 of *Philosophische Bibliothek.* Edited by Rothert Hans-Joachim. Hamburg: Felix Meiner, 1958.

WORKS BY OTHER AUTHORS

Barth, Karl. *From Rousseau to Ritschl*. London: SCM, 1959.
———. *The Theology of Schleiermacher: Lectures at Göttingen, Winter Semester of 1923/24*. Edited by Dietrich Ritschl. Translated G. W. Bromiley. Grand Rapids: Eerdmans, 1982.
Birkner, Hans-Joachim. *Schleiermachers Christliche Sittenlehre*. Berlin: Toepelmann, 1964.
Brunner, Emil. *Die Mystik und das Wort*. 2nd ed. Tübingen: Mohr, 1928.
Calvin, John. *Institutes of the Christian Religion*. Translated by Henry Beveridge. 2 vols. London: Clarke, 1953.
Dawson, Jerry F. *Friedrich Schleiermacher: The Evolution of a Nationalist*. Austin: University of Texas, 1966.
Dilthey, Wilhelm. *Leben Schleiermachers*. Berlin: Reimer, 1870.
Drummond, Andrew L. *German Protestantism Since Luther*. London: Epworth, 1951.
Duke, James. "Translator's Introduction." In *Hermeneutics: The Handwritten Manuscripts*, edited by Heinz Kimmerle, translated by James Duke and Jack Forstman, 1–18. Atlanta: Scholars, 1986.
Duke, James, and Robert Streetman, eds. *Barth and Schleiermacher: Beyond the Impasse?* Philadelphia: Fortress, 1988.
Flueckiger, Felix. *Philosophie und Theologie bei Schleiermacher*. Zollikon-Zurich: Evangelischer Verlag, 1947.
Funk, Robert W., ed. *Schleiermacher as Contemporary*. Journal for Theology and the Church 7. New York: Herder & Herder, 1970
Gadamer, Hans-Georg. *Truth and Method*. Second Revised Edition. Translated by Joel Weinsheimer and Donald G. Marshall. New York: Continuum, 1995.
———. *Wahrheit und Methode: Grundzuege einer philosophischen Hermeneutik*. Tübingen: Mohr, 1960.
Galling, Kurt, ed. *Die Religion in Geschichte und Gegenwart*. 6 vols. Tübingen: Mohr, 1957–62.
Hagan, Anette I. *Eternal Blessedness for All: A Historical-Systematic Examination of Schleiermacher's Understanding of Predestination*. Princeton Theological Monograph Series. Eugene, OR: Pickwick, 2013.
Heidegger, Martin. "Phenomenological Interpretations in Connection with Aristotle: An Indication of the Hermeneutical Situation." In *Supplements: From the Earliest Essays to Being and Time and Beyond*, edited by John van Buren, translated by John van Buren, 111–45. Albany: State University of New York Press, 2002.
Herzog, Frederick. "Schleiermacher's Hermeneutics." ThM diss., Princeton University, 1950.
———. "The Possibility of Theological Understanding: An Inquiry into the Presuppositions of Hermeneutics in Theology." ThD diss., Princeton University, 1953.
Johnson, Robert C. *Authority in Protestant Theology*. Philadelphia: Westminster, 1959.
Kraeling, Emil G. *The Old Testament Since the Reformation*. London: Lutterworth, 1955.
Lietzmann, Hans, ed. *Die Bekenntnisschriften der evangelisch-Lutherischen Kirche*. Göttingen: Vandenhoeck & Ruprecht, 1956.
Loeffler, Paul. "Selbstbewusstaein und Selbstverstaendnis als theologische Prinzipien bei Schleiermacher und Bultmann." *Kerygma und Dogma II* (1956) 304–15.
Mackintosh, H. R. *Types of Modern Theology*. London: Nisbet, 1937.

M'Giffert, Arthur C. *Protestant Thought Before Kant.* New York: Scribner's Sons, 1919.

Munro, Robert. *Schleiermacher: Personal and Speculative.* London: Gardner, 1903.

Niebuhr, Richard R. *Schleiermacher on Christ and Religion.* New York: Scribner's Sons, 1946.

Redeker, Martin. *Schleiermacher: Life and Thought.* Translated by John Wallhausser. Philadelphia: Fortress, 1973

Ritschl, Dietrich. "Editor's Preface." In *The Theology of Schleiermacher: Lectures at Göttingen, Winter Semester of 1923/24,* by Karl Barth, ix–xii. Edited by Dietrich Ritschl. Translated G. W. Bromiley. Grand Rapids: Eerdmans, 1982.

Robinson, James M., and John B. Cobb, eds. *The New Hermeneutic.* New York: Harper & Row, 1964.

Sykes, Stephen. *Friedrich Schleiermacher.* London: Lutterworth, 1971.

Tice, Terrence N. *Schleiermacher Bibliography.* Princeton: Princeton University Press, 1966.

Wilburn, Ralph G. "The Role of Tradition in Schleiermacher's Theology." *Encounter* 23.3 (1962) 300–15.

www.ingramcontent.com/pod-product-compliance
Lightning Source LLC
Chambersburg PA
CBHW051110160426
43193CB00010B/1386